HORRIBLE SCIENCE

BODY OWNER'S HANDBOOK

NICK ARNOLD

illustrated by
TONY DE SAULLES

■ SCHOLASTIC

KU-547-808

Scholastic Children's Books,
Euston House, 24 Eversholt Street,
London NW1 1DB, UK

A division of Scholastic Ltd
London ~ New York ~ Toronto ~ Sydney ~ Auckland
Mexico City ~ New Delhi ~ Hong Kong

First published in the UK by Scholastic Ltd, 2002
This edition published 2009

Text copyright © Nick Arnold, 2002
Illustrations copyright © Tony De Saulles, 2002

ISBN 978 1407 10612 0

Printed and bound by CPI Group (UK) Ltd, Croydon, CR0 4YY

10 9

The right of Nick Arnold and Tony De Saulles to be identified as the author and
illustrator of this work respectively has been asserted by them in accordance
with the Copyright, Designs and Patents Act, 1988.

CONTENTS

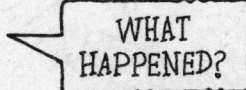
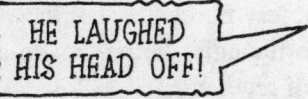

WHAT HAPPENED?

HE LAUGHED HIS HEAD OFF!

Nick Arnold has been writing stories and books since he was a youngster, but never dreamt he'd find fame writing a handbook for body owners. His research involved getting to grips with preserved body bits, studying snot and examining ear wax and he enjoyed every minute of it.

When he's not delving into Horrible Science, he spends his spare time eating pizza, riding his bike and thinking up corny jokes (though not all at the same time).

Tony De Saulles picked up his crayons when he was still in nappies and has been doodling ever since. He takes Horrible Science very seriously and even agreed to test cures for baldness. Fortunately, he has made a full recovery.

When he's not out with his sketchpad, Tony likes to write poetry and play squash, though he hasn't written any poetry about squash yet.

INTRODUCTION

You and I and everyone on Planet Earth have something in common. Each of us owns an incredible walking, talking machine. Know what I mean? It's the human body! That's right – each one of us is a *human body owner*! And that's where our problems begin…

You see, the human body needs lots of looking after, but there's no user guide to show us what to do! No wonder body problems cause such grief! Wouldn't it be *brilliant* if there was a helpful handbook with advice on basic body repairs and avoiding body breakdowns?

Well, now there is! And guess what? You're actually reading it! So, WELCOME TO THE WORLD'S FIRST BODY OWNER'S HANDBOOK!

Of course, there are lots of different human bodies. Just walk down the road and you're sure to see many bodies in all shapes and sizes, ages and states of repair...

But this handbook is designed for every body around today – and that includes *your* body!

So read on and find out how to get the very best from your body. Check out what's right for it, and what isn't. See what each body bit does and how to tackle body breakdown problems. Find out everything you wanted to know about your body and never dared to ask – and more!

But be warned, this handbook won't flinch from foul facts just because they're gruesome and grisly.

It's going to get *right under your body's skin*…

BODY BITS FOR BEGINNERS

In a moment, we'll be looking inside your body to check out its amazing working bits in all their gory glory. But first … CONGRATULATIONS ON OWNING THE BEST BODY MACHINE IN THE UNIVERSE! It really is: for once the adverts are spot-on…

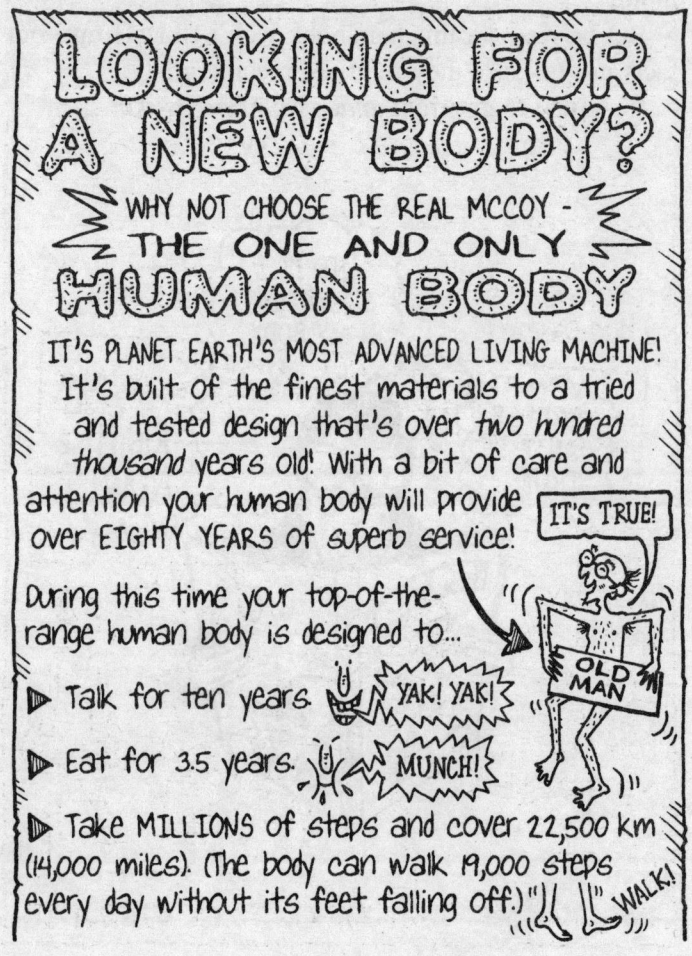

LOOKING FOR A NEW BODY?

WHY NOT CHOOSE THE REAL MCCOY –
THE ONE AND ONLY
HUMAN BODY

IT'S PLANET EARTH'S MOST ADVANCED LIVING MACHINE! It's built of the finest materials to a tried and tested design that's over *two hundred thousand* years old! With a bit of care and attention your human body will provide over EIGHTY YEARS of superb service!

IT'S TRUE!

OLD MAN

During this time your top-of-the-range human body is designed to…

▷ Talk for ten years. YAK! YAK!

▷ Eat for 3.5 years. MUNCH!

▷ Take MILLIONS of steps and cover 22,500 km (14,000 miles). (The body can walk 19,000 steps every day without its feet falling off.) WALK!

8

FLEX!

▶ Bend and straighten its fingers 25 million times without needing new knuckles.

PUMP!

▶ Beat its heart blood-pump over 2.5 billion times non-stop at an average 73 beats a minute, 105,120 beats a day. (Every 24 hours the heart pumps 8 to 16,000 litres of blood and never goes pop!)

THINK!

▶ Store ONE MILLION bits of data in its brain memory - everything from science facts to shopping lists, plus your friends' birthdays, 100,000 words, all the players in your favourite team - and it can recognize over 2,000 faces!

~THE SMALL PRINT~
Remember, the body is designed to do these things over its lifetime. Body owners shouldn't expect their bodies to do them all non-stop!

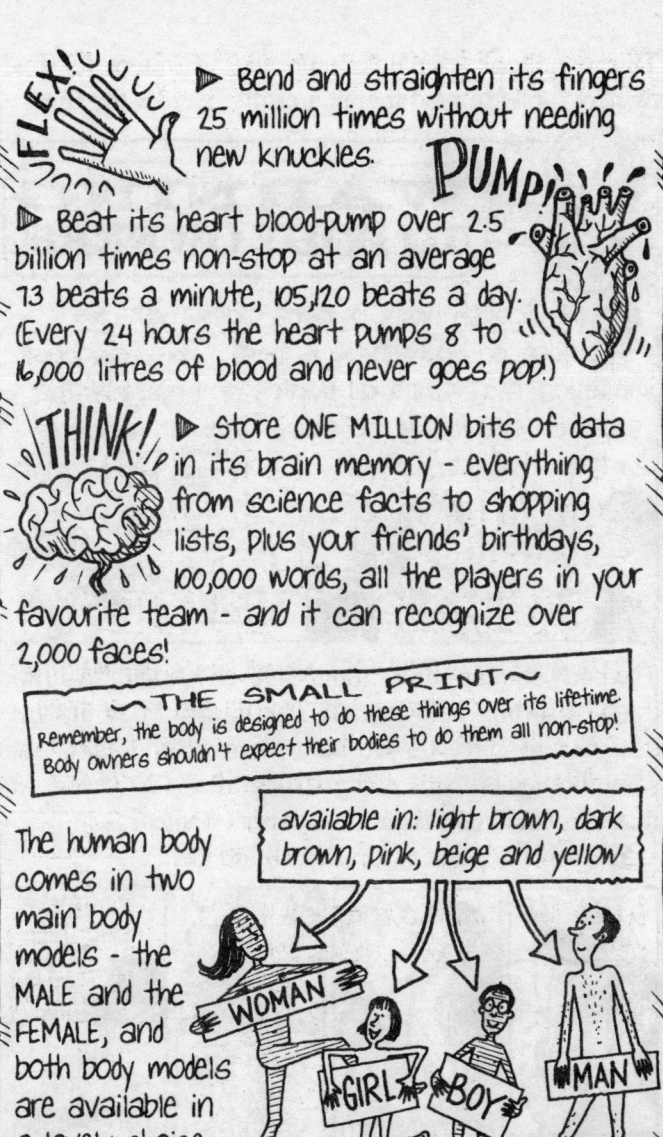

available in: light brown, dark brown, pink, beige and yellow

The human body comes in two main body models - the MALE and the FEMALE, and both body models are available in a lovely choice of colours!

WOMAN   GIRL   BOY   MAN

THE HUMAN BODY - BET YOU CAN'T LIVE WITHOUT IT!

This handbook contains important warnings for body owners – please read them carefully. Here's the first:

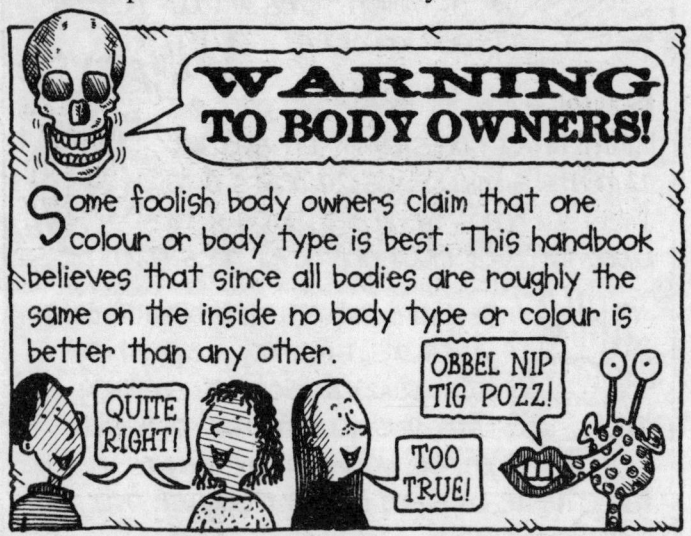

The body sounds pretty impressive, eh? And did you spot the best selling point of all? The human body has been designed to carry on working for over *80 years* – and some bodies are still going strong after 120 years! And that's *loads* longer than most animal bodies...

• Sparrows hop the twig after 18 months.

• Dormice are dead as doornails after five years.
• Swans sing their swan-songs after seven years.

- Dogs bow-wow out after ten years.
- Cats come a cropper after 15 years.

But body owners may be disappointed to learn that their human body won't last as long as some animal bodies…
- The oldest tortoise plodded on for 150 years.
- Sharks and lobsters seem to go on and on without showing signs of age until they're finished off by other animals.

Mind you, 99.9% of human body owners wouldn't swap their bodies for anything else. I mean, who'd want a body that lumbers around eating lettuce all day?

Well, now you've found out how amazing your body is, I bet you're itching to take a peep at the working bits inside. Don't worry, this is quite normal. *But DON'T do it!* The body isn't designed to be opened by non-experts and this can result in serious body breakdowns!

LEAVE THE CUTTING TO US!

For example, in 1994 a French postman cut open his body to check that body mechanics (also called surgeons) had removed a body bit called the appendix. The poor old postman's body broke down for ever.

What that postie needed was a body-bit checklist with details of what each body part is designed to do. Then he might have found out what was going on inside his body without looking inside. Well, as luck would have it, this handbook features just such a checklist and it's coming up next...

THE BODY-BIT CHECKLIST

All the body bits pictured below were supplied by our scientific expert, the one and only madly famous, famously mad scientist – Baron Frankenstein. It seems the Baron has quite a collection…

How horribly charming to meet you!

THE INCREDIBLE STRETCHY BODY COVERING

The first thing you notice when you look at your body is the super-stretchy outer-body cover (also known as the skin). The skin is a self-cooling germ-proof wrap-around coating designed to protect the delicate body bits inside.

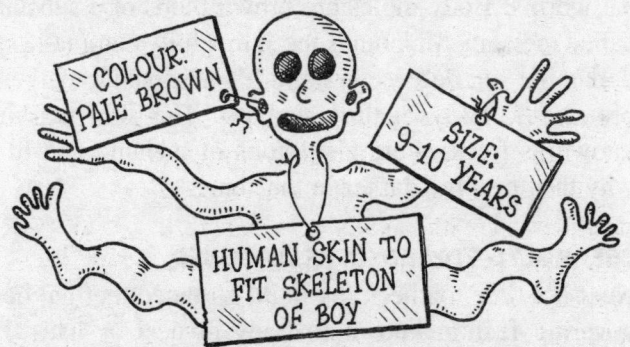

COLOUR: PALE BROWN

SIZE: 9-10 YEARS

HUMAN SKIN TO FIT SKELETON OF BOY

The skin is programmed to replace itself when it's worn out and it even repairs itself when damaged. But it's got one annoying design defect. Worn-out skin flakes off over the carpet. During its lifetime the body sheds 47.6 kg of waste skin. That's equal to *one thousand* layers of skin or *five* bulging rubbish sacks!

The skin is only 0.5 mm thick, but it's surprisingly big and baggy. If you stripped the skin off a large male body and rolled it flat (a messy job, so you'd best not try it!) the skin would cover up to two square metres. This skin weighs about the same as three winter overcoats.

If you look closely at your body you might spot a few moles. NO, not those funny underground animals that eat worms! Body moles are brown blobs of a substance called melanin. Melanin is the skin's fully automatic self-darkening sun-defence system. It's designed to darken to protect the body against sunburn. The skin markings known as freckles are also blobs of melanin and that's why they become darker in the sun.

THE MULTI-STRANDED HEAD COVER

Next it's time to check the multi-stranded thermal head-covering feature known to body owners as hair. This body part is made up of about 100,000 hairs (older bodies may have less – see page 135 for the bald facts).

Each hair is squeezed from a tiny pit on the head at a

speed of 1 cm per month. In a year, a human body makes 12 km of the stuff – about 1,000 km in an average body lifetime or enough hair to stretch from London to Paris by road and back again. If the hair wasn't cut and didn't fall out, it would grow hair, there and everywhere…

WATER-DEFLECTORS

These strange hairy caterpillar-like objects, commonly known as eyebrows, are designed to stop sweat from the body's automatic water-cooling system trickling down into the eyes.

You'll be shocked to know, dear reader, that your human body has more hairs than a chimpanzee! The only reason your body doesn't look like King Kong is because its hairs are finer and shorter and harder to see.

BODY LANGUAGE

Body owners may find it useful to understand the jargon used by experts. Don't worry, this handbook will supply you with enough word power to stagger a body expert (also known as a scientist).

How would you feel if your body has rutilism (ru-til-lis-m)?

I'M PROUD OF IT!

Answer:

Quite right! Rutilism is the body expert's word for *red hair*. Red hair contains iron and the red colour is caused by a rusting effect! Other hair colours are caused by the amount of melanin they contain, but auburn hair is a mix of red hair and melanin. By the way, body owners, red hair might be "rusty," but it doesn't squeak – so put that oil can down!

BUILT-IN FINGER AND TOE PROTECTORS

Every body is equipped with tough finger and toe protectors called nails. The body has been programmed to automatically replace its nails over time. Every day the fingernails get longer by the width of two hairs and if you

GROW!

16

didn't cut these nails your body would produce 28 metres of nails during its life-time!

NOSE PICKING IS A BIT TRICKY THESE DAYS

Newer bodies produce nails faster than older bodies – especially if the nails are nibbled. Tut tut!

THE CENTRAL INFORMATION PROCESSING UNIT

The body's top-of-the-range highly advanced information processing unit is known as the brain. In order to function properly the brain needs to be kept warmer than the rest of the body and it also consumes up to 20% of the body's fuel (known as food) – that's more than any other body part. The brain also needs 16 times more oxygen (the gas your body takes from the air) than any other body bit.

As a body owner you don't need to know the details of how the brain works (scientists are still puzzling over some of these), but it helps to have some idea of what's going on in there. Baron Frankenstein has kindly chopped a spare brain in half so we can see the main bits. Thanks, Baron!

YOU'RE WELCOME!

CEREBRUM

Plans and controls body movements and vital sensory data-processing such as vision and sound detection. It's designed to solve problems and store data in its memory.

CEREBELLUM

Controls body actions that can be done without the brain planning them, like riding a bike. But not *brainless* body behaviour like making rude noises to show off.

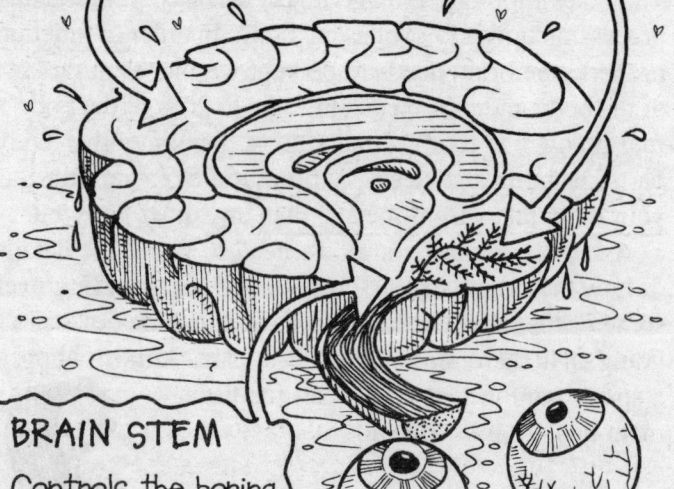

BRAIN STEM

Controls the boring but vital jobs like breathing air and digesting food.

A failure of these systems needs emergency breakdown treatment. If you notice your body trying to breathe food, you'll need a body mechanic fast (see page 85 – choking.)

Every day your body automatically produces half a glass of brain juice for the brain to float around in. This watery stuff cushions the brain inside its protection shield (or skull, as it's called). And every day some brain juice oozes back into the blood – you might call this a fluid situation, ha ha!

BODY LANGUAGE

A body expert says…

YOU'VE GOT A BLUE SPOT…

Do you say…

NO, THEY'RE RED WITH WHITE BITS IN THE MIDDLE!

Answer:
No, the body really does have a blue spot … in its *brain!* The blue spot pumps out a chemical that powers up the brain when anything interesting happens to grab the brain's attention. Stuff like learning a really cool fact or spotting a hungry-looking dinosaur. So now for some interesting info to get that blue spot squirting…

Body data

The brain uses 13% less energy watching TV than it does when it's doing nothing! No wonder some bodies look like dribbling zombies after watching the shopping channel for a few hours.

The more the body practises a task, the better the brain becomes at controlling the movements needed. For example, if a body plays an instrument, it develops the area of the brain that deals with music. I also enjoy music — especially playing the church organ madly at the dead of night, ha ha!

THE FULLY AUTOMATED BLOOD PUMP AND AIR INLET/EXHAUST SYSTEM

Along with the brain, the fully automated long-life blood pump, or heart, is the body's most vital part. It's basically a non-stop fluid-flow control booster powerful enough to pump all the body's blood around the whole body every minute. But in fact, it can do this heart-thumping good job in just ten seconds!

Listen well, dear reader: the bigger the body, the slower the heartbeat. An elephant heart beats more slowly than the human heart, which beats more slowly than a cat heart. Indeed, I should know — I've cut out a good many hearts in my time!

Lungs are the body's self-regulating air inlet and exhaust system. They're designed to take oxygen from the air into the blood, and puff out waste carbon dioxide gas (you can find out why this is important on page 86).

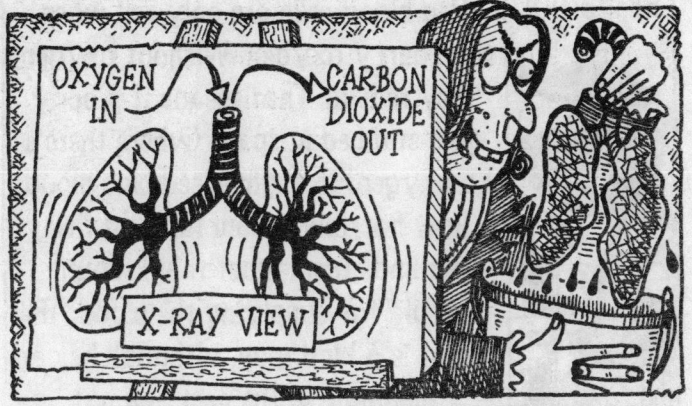

THE INTERNAL FLUID TRANSPORTATION SYSTEM

The body's blood supply is a state-of-the-art fluid transport system. And although it looks like a gloopy red liquid, your body's five litres (8.8 pints) of blood are swarming with tiny red and white blood cells! Each of these units functions like a micro-engineered robot with a job to do inside the body. Red blood cells carry oxygen through the blood tubes known as blood vessels and white blood cells fight germs.

Body data
Unlike other machines, your body machine may be attacked by microbes. Harmful microbes are known as germs and they can multiply inside the body and destroy its cells. This is a major body design problem, but you'll be relieved to know that your body has been programmed to defend itself (see page 104 for the details).

Blood also carries food to the body bits. The body has 96,000 km of blood vessels. (You may wonder how they all fit in – it's bleeding amazing!)

RED BLOOD CELLS

Red blood cells are only red when they carry oxygen. Without oxygen, they're blue. That means if a body gets stabbed in space (where there's no oxygen) it might bleed blue blood. How horribly colourful! And that reminds me, I must thank Count Dracula for supplying the blood. The Count is a kind man, although he can be a pain in the neck, ha ha!

THE FUEL STORAGE TANK AND CONVEYOR BELT

This system (often known as the stomach and guts) breaks food down into chemicals that can enter the blood and fuel the body. Body experts call this digestion and describe the stomach and guts as the digestive system. Each day the guts process ten litres of sloppy, half-digested food. And this fully automated 24-hour operation also handles liquid fuels (known as drinks).

The system works by pumping out chemically engineered digestive juices such as spit that help to break food chemicals up. The juices are made in special production units called glands and squirted out automatically. Spit, for example, squirts into the food entry hatch, or mouth as body owners call it.

The body's fully automated guts are designed to shift half-digested food by about 2.8 cm per minute. And, as every body owner knows, unused body food is ejected from the rear-end gas vent/solid-waste ejection pipe after about 24 hours.

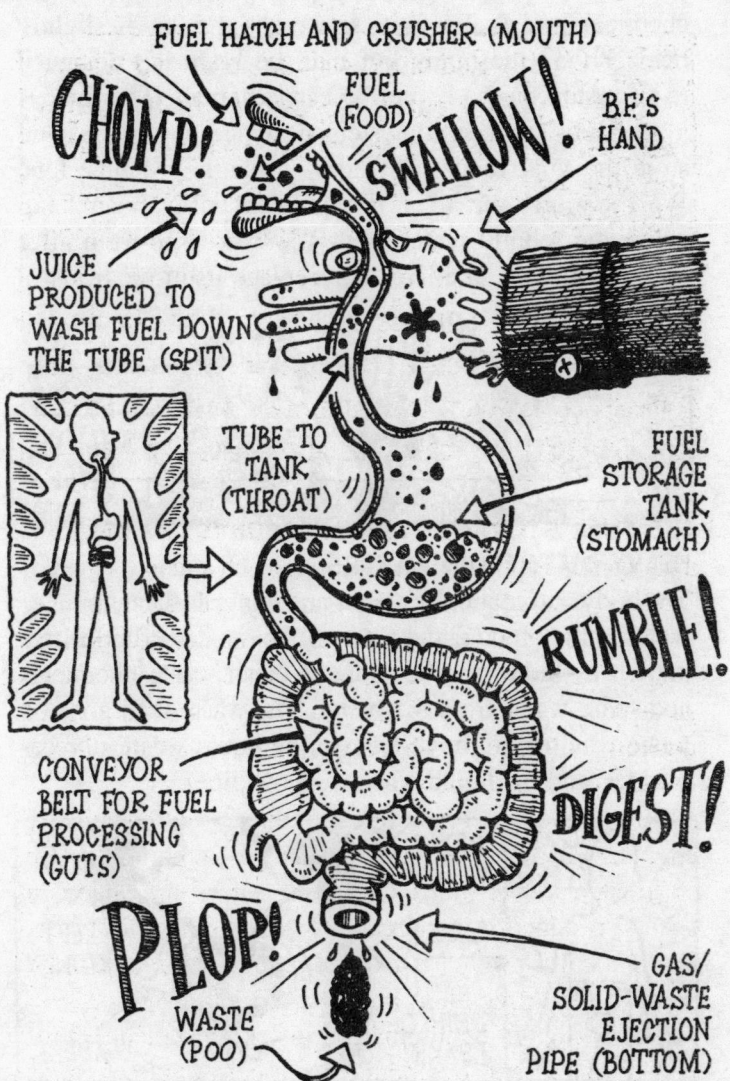

FUEL HATCH AND CRUSHER (MOUTH)

CHOMP!

FUEL (FOOD)

SWALLOW!

BE'S HAND

JUICE PRODUCED TO WASH FUEL DOWN THE TUBE (SPIT)

TUBE TO TANK (THROAT)

FUEL STORAGE TANK (STOMACH)

RUMBLE!

CONVEYOR BELT FOR FUEL PROCESSING (GUTS)

DIGEST!

PLOP!

WASTE (POO)

GAS/ SOLID-WASTE EJECTION PIPE (BOTTOM)

THE MULTI-FUNCTIONAL FOOD AND CHEMICAL PROCESSOR

The liver is the body's fully portable multi-functional chemical processing unit. It weighs 1.5 kg – slightly heavier than the brain, but like the brain it's designed to fit inside the body and be carried about. The liver is a precisely engineered system designed to sort out and store the vital food substances – sugars, proteins, fats. What's more, the liver is equipped with an amazing automatic rebuild feature that allows it to re-form after damage. In fact, the liver can replace itself from just a sliver of liver!

HEAVY-DUTY FLUID FILTERS

The body automatically cleans and controls the amount of water in the blood using a pair of heavy-duty fluid filters known as kidneys. The kidneys clean waste chemicals and spare water from the blood. The waste then goes on a one-way trip to the toilet (via the liquid waste store or bladder, and the liquid waste outflow pipe).

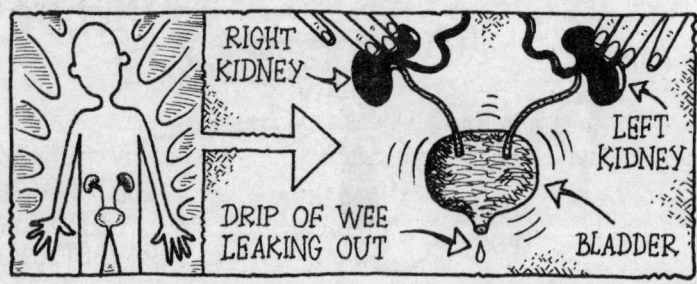

Every day the kidneys check every drop of blood 36 times and produce 1.5 litres of yellow body waste or pee as it's often called. That's 40,000 litres in your body's life – enough to fill four road tankers!

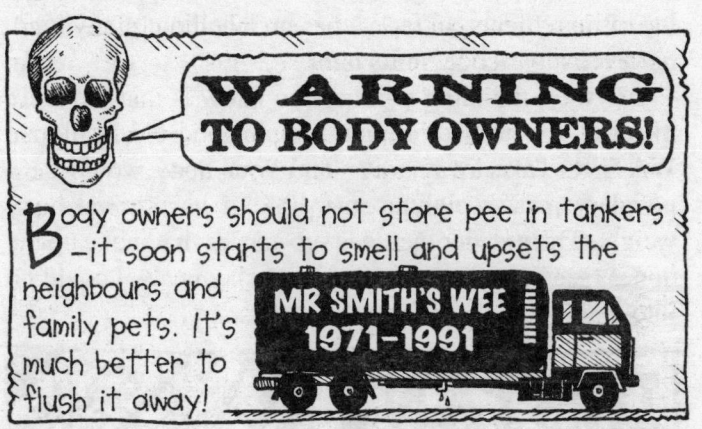

WARNING TO BODY OWNERS!

Body owners should not store pee in tankers –it soon starts to smell and upsets the neighbours and family pets. It's much better to flush it away!

MR SMITH'S WEE 1971–1991

Well, the author may think that urine (the proper name for liquid waste) should be flushed away. But I think it's an excellent gargle and mouthwash! I'll tell you more on page 107. Cheers!

Body data
One really revolting pee ingredient is called urea. This chemical contains poisonous ammonia from waste protein. If it builds up it can cause a total body breakdown. That's why your body is so desperate to get rid of it. Urea also turns up in skin, and hair and nails. Yes, it's in fingernails – now that really is something to chew over!

BUILDING BLOCKS FOR BODY BITS

At this point all you body owners out there may be wondering what kind of substance your body's skin and brain and kidneys and body bits are actually *made of*. Well, rather confusingly, your body isn't supplied with a list of ingredients. In fact, it has no labelling of any kind, not even a bar code on its bum...

Anyway, the thing you need to know is that the main material of your body is plain simple good-old-fashioned WATER. Take away water and your body would be a powdery mass weighing just 40% of its original body weight. The powder includes substances that make up the bones (see page 29) and other vital chemicals. I could go into details but these facts are rather *dry*...

Most of your body's complicated chemicals are arranged in tiny self-contained self-replacing micro-engineered units known as cells. Do you remember the red and white blood cells on page 21? Here are some more body cells as seen through a powerful microscope. In fact, your body has 100,000,000,000,000 (one hundred thousand BILLION) cells, er – give or take a few billion.

Hey, body owners – stop right there! Let's take a deep breath and *think* about that number. Even *one million* is a horribly huge figure. In 1982, Australian Les Stewart decided to type every number from one to one million (don't ask me why). It took him *sixteen years* and 19,990 sheets of paper. But at that rate it would take Les over *one hundred million years* to number the cells in his own body! And by then he'd have run out of fingers to count with

A cell is too tiny to see without a microscope and yet it's as complex as a small city. But amazingly your body automatically produces *one billion cells* every hour. They're needed to make the body increase in size (young bodies are designed to do this) and to replace cells that break down. In just one day your body makes more cells than there are human bodies on Earth! No wonder smaller bodies get worn out at school!

The programme of replacing cells is vital to keep the body on the road. Here's a typical body cell breakdown-and-replacement job sheet...

THE BODY REPAIR SHOP

CELL-REPLACEMENT SCHEDULE

Check when cells need replacing. Fit new ones as and when the old ones break down...

✱ Red blood cells should keep going for six months without too much bother.

✱ Liver cells "liver" for five months, ha ha! Just keep an eye on them...

✱ Skin cells last three to four weeks – replace them to keep bodywork in good condition.

✱ Stomach, gut and mouth cells last for just three days – these will need constant work, tut tut!

✱ Check cells that produce new bone – they're supposed to make a new skeleton body frame every seven years to replace lost bone cells.

IF WE DON'T DO THESE JOBS IT COSTS THE BODY OWNER AN ARM AND A LEG! MIND YOU WE CAN'T REPLACE LOST TEETH OR KIDNEY TUBES OR MOST BRAIN CELLS, AND WE CAN'T PUT NEW EGGS INTO A FEMALE BODY (SEE PAGE 142). NONE OF THESE ARE DESIGNED TO BE REPLACED. YOU JUST CAN'T GET THE PARTS, GUV.

So prepare yourself for a shock. That means… Most of your body bits are less than *ten years old*! Even battered old bodies are mostly *no older* than a good-condition ten-year-old body! You can find out why older bodies look so ancient on page 132, but right now we've got to finish off the checklist…

BODY FRAMEWORK AND MOTORS

Your body's super-strong support framework (often called the skeleton) is designed to stop it flopping all over the floor. It's actually made of 206 interconnected units called bones made of a unique high-endurance mixture of calcium and phosphate chemicals with added protein called collagen. The skeleton weighs 9 kg and it's been engineered to carry five times its own weight without breaking.

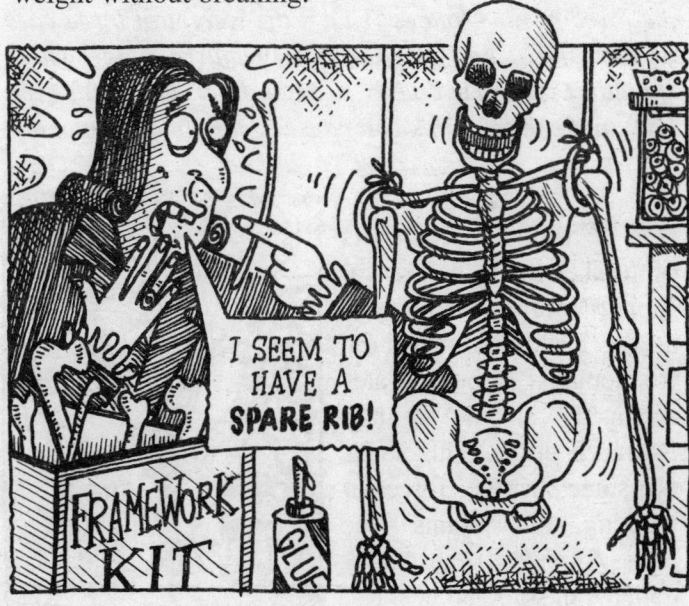

Bones are often connected by shock-absorbers called joints. The joint shock-absorbers protect the body by cushioning the bones in bags of squishy fluid. The ends of the bones themselves are coated in a soft shock-absorbing substance called cartilage. This protection is vital because the joints take a lot of wear and tear – an ankle joint bears the force of TEN TIMES your body's weight every time it hops. Yet the joint is strong enough to help your body take millions of steps without squeaking or going rusty.

Body data

1 When your body does a sit-up exercise, its lower backbone carries the same weight as 174 metres of water crushing a diver.
2 When your body lands after a high jump, its bones take the force of nine tonnes. That's the weight of three cars or one and a half elephants. (Obviously body owners shouldn't test their body's strength by trying to lift even half an elephant – this can cause severe body damage!)

One of the most vital parts of the skeleton is the vertical support column (also known as the backbone or spine). It's actually 33 bony plates arranged in a springy S-shaped curve. This soaks up some of the force of walking, but strains (see pages 67 and 68) cause back damage in some bodies.

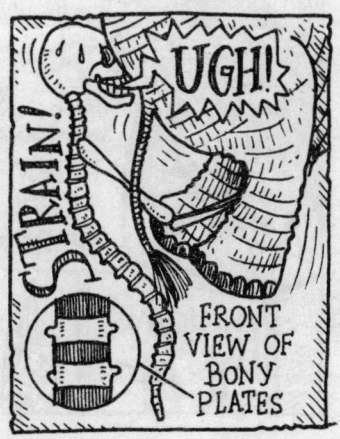

STRAIN! UGH!

FRONT VIEW OF BONY PLATES

Body data

1 Can your body crack its knuckles? Do its ankle joints click, or its knees creak when the legs straighten? These odd sounds are perfectly normal – and believe it or not they're made by bubbles. Normally, bubbles of nitrogen gas are dissolved in the liquid that cushions the joints. They're like bubbles in fizzy lemonade before you open it.

2 When the joint is forced apart, bubbles appear as the pressure is released, just like when you open that lemonade. The bubbles pop and you hear a cracking noise. Let's hope your body's joints don't start burping afterwards.

HIGH-PERFORMANCE MOTOR POWER UNITS

The body's power-unit motors are known as muscles. All you body owners out there might be amazed to learn that every body has over 600 muscles. They're controlled by nerve signals from the brain and pull on the bones with extra-tough cables called tendons. (Nerves are the body's high-tech telephone wires for messages to and from the brain.)

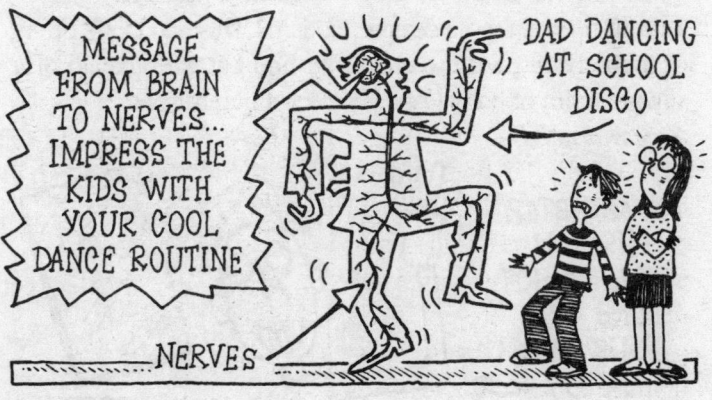

MESSAGE FROM BRAIN TO NERVES... IMPRESS THE KIDS WITH YOUR COOL DANCE ROUTINE

DAD DANCING AT SCHOOL DISCO

NERVES

After much toil I have put together all the body bits to make a monster. And I've brought him to life in order to prove that smiling is easier than frowning...

WHEN THE MONSTER SMILES HE USES 17 MUSCLES,

BUT WHEN HE FROWNS HE USES 43!

FROWN!

Don't wear your muscles out!

TEST YOUR BODY 1: JUST NOSING AROUND

Is your body up to its design standard? This handbook offers you, the body owner, a chance to find out with the aid of a unique series of body tests. Here's test number one.

You will need:

A MONSTER (IF YOU HAVEN'T GOT ONE, USE YOUR OWN BODY)

A MIRROR

What you do:
1 Get your body to wrinkle its nose, like so…

2 Now try to do it without moving its upper lip…

You should find:
It's impossible for the body to wrinkle its nose without lifting its upper lip. This is because the same muscle controls both movements.

What an uplifting test! But then your body's muscle engineering is incredibly impressive – yes it is, body owners – even if your body is fitted with low-power mini-muscles.

But I'm sorry to say that your human body doesn't measure up too well against some animal bodies. Few human bodies have ever managed to move at more than 43.5 km (27 miles) per hour – and only for a few seconds. But that's just a gentle jog for some creatures. Cheetahs chase about at 101 km (62.75 miles) per hour – and if an ant grew as big as your body, it would power through your picnic at 150 km (93 miles) per hour! Ant that amazin', body owners?

A MESSAGE TO BODY OWNERS...

Not every body can reach the body's top speed, but if your body is more of a tired tortoise than a charging cheetah, don't despair! Your body is still a high-tech machine with awesome automatic features that would turn a robot green with envy. Well, that's if robots *could* turn green! Anyway, you'd best read on and check if your body's auto-systems are working...

GREEN!

YES, READ ON, BODY OWNERS, BLUB!

AUTOMATIC BODY FEATURES

Your body has been designed to suck in air, sense its surroundings and protect itself from dirt and dust. And the really amazing thing about these features is that they're *fully automatic*. So that means you, the body owner, don't have to switch them on in the morning. Let's begin with...

THE AUTOMATIC AIR INLET/EXHAUST SYSTEM

A vital automatic function (known as breathing) supplies the body with oxygen from the air. Without it your body would suffer total breakdown in *three minutes*. But since the breathing function is always switched on, you can relax and forget about it.

Mind you, the breathing function is so amazingly designed that body experts get quite breathless about it! Your body pulls down a sheet of muscle under the lungs called the diaphragm (dia-fram) whilst pulling its ribcage up and out...

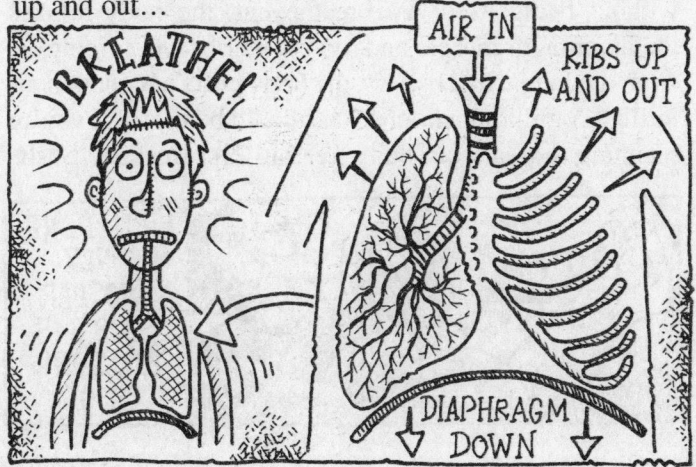

Air rushes down the gas feeder tube (known as the windpipe) into the lungs. When the body isn't active, the best way for it to breathe is through the airborne chemical sampling chamber (or nose space) – the entrance nozzles are often known as nostrils.

NOSE BREATHING PROCEDURE

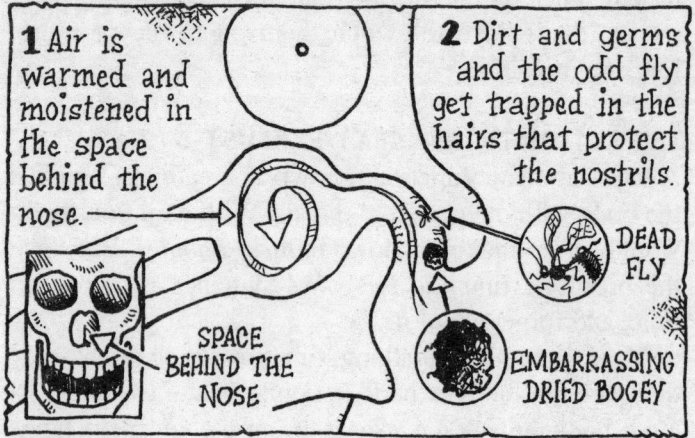

1 Air is warmed and moistened in the space behind the nose.

2 Dirt and germs and the odd fly get trapped in the hairs that protect the nostrils.

DEAD FLY

SPACE BEHIND THE NOSE

EMBARRASSING DRIED BOGEY

Oddly enough, 30% of the body's air is breathed out without being used. To breathe out, the body relaxes the diaphragm muscle and lowers its ribcage, forcing air from the lungs. In 21 years, the body puffs out enough air to fill 3.5 million balloons. This could be useful if you're planning to treat your body to a big 21st Birthday Bash.

WELL DONE, ONLY ANOTHER 1,278,645 BALLOONS TO GO!

One really odd form of breathing is yawning. The body yawns:

a) When it's feeling tired.

b) During boring science lessons.

No one knows why bodies yawn, but it could be some sort of signal because when one body yawns others often join in. Does looking at this picture make your body yawn…?

I said … oh no, I told you it was catching!

KEEPING THE VITAL TUBES CLEAR

Some dust and germs and bits of that trapped fly may get past the nostril hairs or get sucked into the mouth during breathing. Fortunately, the body has yet another automatic protection system to catch them. In this handbook it's known as the AWESOMELY INCREDIBLE SNOT CONVEYOR BELT. Here's how it works…

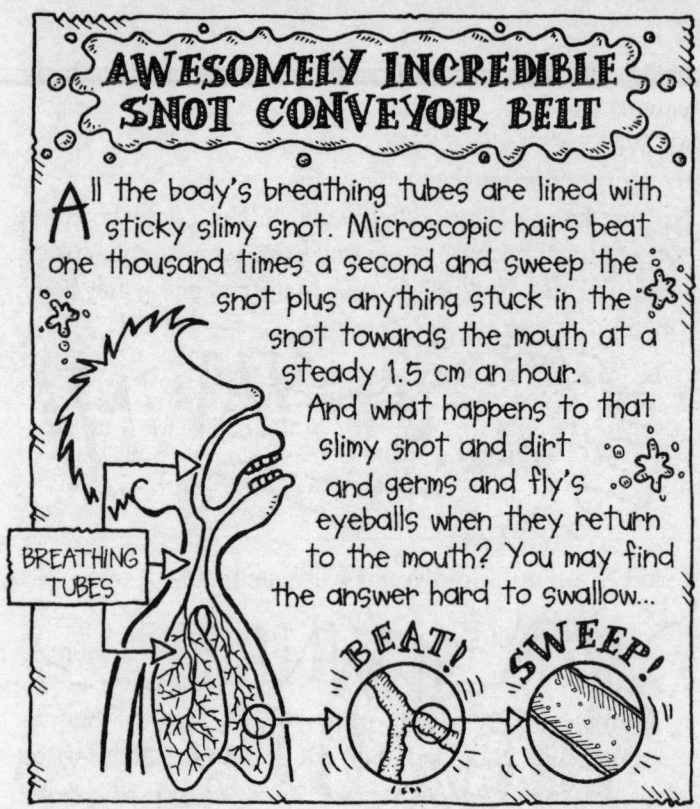

AWESOMELY INCREDIBLE SNOT CONVEYOR BELT

All the body's breathing tubes are lined with sticky slimy snot. Microscopic hairs beat one thousand times a second and sweep the snot plus anything stuck in the snot towards the mouth at a steady 1.5 cm an hour.

And what happens to that slimy snot and dirt and germs and fly's eyeballs when they return to the mouth? You may find the answer hard to swallow...

BREATHING TUBES

BEAT!

SWEEP!

And now for the first in our exclusive series of real-life stories that show the body in action.

CURIOUS CASE STUDY: DANGEROUS DRIBBLING

Some bodies spit: that means they fire gooey globs of spit at high speed from their mouth food-entry hatches. All body owners must be warned against this horrible habit! In 1977, French body owner Claude Antoine practised long-range spitting whilst hurling his body across the room. Unfortunately, when he reached an upper window, he couldn't stop. Claude's battered body needed a long stay in a body-repair facility (often referred to as a hospital).

BODY LANGUAGE

A body expert announces:

I'M STUDYING MUCUS

Do you say…

C-O-O-L! I LURVE MUSIC. HAVE YOU HEARD THE NEW NUMBER ONE?

Answer:
No. Mucus is the body expert's name for snot – and it's also found in spit.

If anything bigger than a microbe gets into the body's breathing tubes, the body activates its automatic particle ejection programme – this is known as sneezing or coughing. Sneezing gets rid of anything that upsets the sensitive upper throat area such as dust.

SNIFF!

A-A-A A-A CHOO!

And coughing splutters out any nasty stuff that falls further down the windpipe.

Body data

1 In 1635, Dr William Lee announced that sneezing was caused by the sun's heat drawing moisture from the brain into the nose. But today's body experts are quite snotty about this idea.

2 The World Sneezing Record is held by a 12-year-old British girl who sneezed for TWO AND HALF YEARS from 1981 to 1983. She atishoo'ed ONE MILLION times a year – an achievement not to be sniffed at.

3 Contrary to what your friends might tell you, if a body sneezes with its eyes open its eyeballs DON'T plop out. Strong muscles hold the body's eyeballs in their sockets. The eyelids close automatically to stop blood vessels in the eyeballs breaking – and making the eye appear bloodshot.

And whilst we're talking about eyes, let's spot another range of automatic body features: the sensory data-collection systems – including, of course, the visual-input system…

AUTOMATIC SENSORY EQUIPMENT

The body receives visual data through two high-tech light receptors known as eyeballs. This process is known as seeing. Each eyeball weighs seven g and is designed to sense light falling on millions of light-sensitive cells in the retina area at the back of each eyeball. The retina fires data to the brain via a high-speed cable of two million nerve fibres.

AUTOMATIC EYE-WASHING FEATURE

Body owners may like to know that their body is equipped with a unique automatic eye-washing feature. The eyeballs are protected by loose skin covers or eyelids. The eyelids close automatically – it's called blinking – and each time this happens they wash the eyeballs with a cleaning fluid known as tears.

Actually, all you body owners reading this might like to know that different sorts of tears are designed to form protective layers over eyeballs. There's a layer of gooey snotty tears (with mucus) on the eyeball's surface. Above this you'll find ordinary tears, and on top are oily tears that stop the other tears drying up. Yes, tears are so good it would be a crying shame if you ever ran out of them!

Blinking takes place about ten to 24 times a minute, or about 415 million times in a body's lifetime. If the body is damaged, it blinks more often, and if the body is just ticking over, or reading, it blinks less, as these photos of the Monster will prove...

MONSTER READING A HORRIBLE SCIENCE BOOK...

MONSTER SITTING ON A DRAWING PIN...

The tears are pumped out of the tear-production units over the eyes and drain into the corner of each eye nearest the nose and down little tubes to the nose. This can give your body an embarrassing snotty nose at emotional moments. Then, during the night, the tears dry to sleepy dust. Aaah!

Body data
1 Elephants have drippy eyes and crocodiles cry to get rid of salt (yes, there's really such a thing as crocodile tears!), but the human body is the champion tear-jerker.

It squirts out 65 litres of tears in its lifetime – about 1,850,000 tears. That's a huge amount of soggy hankies... There, there!

2 Human bodies cry when their brain processors run complex data programs known as feelings. These might include happy and sad and angry and upset feelings and wanting-attention signals. It all goes to show what strange mixed-up bodies they are.
3 Female bodies cry about six times a month, but male bodies only cry twice a month (at other times they go dewy-eyed in a strong, sensitive, but still rather manly way). And talking about being sensitive...

HIGH-TECH TOUCH-SENSOR SYSTEMS

The body's skin is supplied with millions of inbuilt high-tech micro-sensor units. Some are designed to detect pressure and others are sensitive to temperature changes or lighter touch, and all are linked via nerves to the brain. Here's your chance to test them...

TEST YOUR BODY 2: A TOUCHING MOMENT

You will need:
Your body
A compass or pair of pointed scissors (careful now!)

What you do:

1 Open the compass or scissors until the the points are about 2 mm apart.
2 Close your body's eyes and touch one of its fingertips *gently* with the points.
3 Now open the eyes and touch the bare skin of your body's calf with the points.

You should find:
Your body senses two points touching its finger, but only ONE POINT when the points touch its calf! Fingers are more sensitive than legs because the touch sensors are closer together. Yes, this experiment really does make *sense* – I'm sure you'll see the *point* of it.

SOUND, TASTE AND SCENT-DETECTOR SYSTEMS

The body's audio-detector system registers sounds that are picked up by the external sound-detector dishes (or ears) mounted on each side of the head. The ear mechanism is engineered to turn sounds into nerve signals that go to the brain.

HOUSE WITH SATELLITE DISH

HEAD WITH SOUND DISH

But although the ears collect sound, body owners may be surprised to know that their bodies can detect sounds quite well *without them*. That's why bodies equipped with huge flapping ears aren't better at sound detection than those with smaller ears.

Body data
1 In 1994 a Spanish body owner sliced off his own ears. He was trying to block the sound of his nagging mother-in-law. It made little difference – and no doubt she made some very cutting remarks.
2 Your body's sound-detection system can't make out really high sounds such as bat squeaks. Mind you, some smaller bodies don't seem to hear when they're being ordered to go to bed.

FOOD AND AIRBORNE CHEMICAL SENSOR SYSTEMS
The body's food chemical sensors are based on the tongue – that's the common name for the wobbly extensible probe located in the food-entry hatch and linked by nerves to the brain.

The smell/scent/whiff/pong detecting function is based in the nose space. Here, two stamp-sized sensory units detect airborne chemicals and send nerve signals to the brain. Body owners reading this may like to know that the 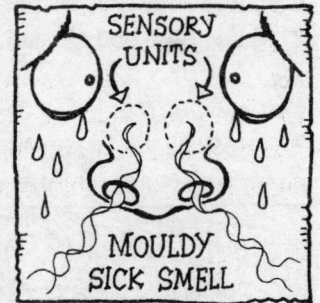 brain's built-in memory files store details of up to TEN THOUSAND smells – including revolting ones. Female noses detect smells better than male noses – bad news for any girl sharing a home with a smelly male body.

The sense of smell switches off if the nose sniffs one smell for hours and hours. I find it horribly hard to detect the odour of rotting flesh unless I take a horrible holiday from work, ha ha!

FLESHY PONG

TEST YOUR BODY 3: THE STRANGE SECRET OF THE NOSTRILS

You will need:
Your body
A mirror

What you do:
1 Lift your body's chin up and use the mirror to take a good hard look up those nostrils – yes, I'm sorry folks, it's all in the name of science!
2 Make your body breathe sharply though its nostrils.

You should find:
The nostrils get bigger as your body takes in air, but one nostril is always slightly wider than the other.

BREATHE IN BREATHE IN

46

The smaller nostril often gets blocked when your body has been attacked by germs and has the disease known as a cold. (A disease is a minor body breakdown caused by germs. See page 106 for the drippy details.)

BODY SCENT DETECTION QUIZ

So how well do you know your own body? Are you a budding body expert or a baffled body beginner? Find out in the first of our series of exclusive body owner's quizzes…

1 Some body advice experts (known as doctors) detect diseases by sniffing the skin. What does gangrene (when the infected body bits rot) smell like?

a) School dinner.
b) Very old fish.
c) Mouldy apples.

2 In 2001, US military planners were working on extra-powerful stink bombs to control riots. In tests, what smell proved the most effective?

a) Poo (that's solid body waste, as if you didn't know!).

b) Sweaty feet smeared with rotting butter.

c) Vomit (ejected body food).

3 In the USA, fir trees are sprayed with a substance to put off thieves. What does this stinking substance smell like?

a) Skunk juice.
b) Fox wee.
c) Bad breath.

4 A sensory analyst is trained to spot dozens of different smells. In one US company women analysts were given a disgusting duty. Did they have to…?

a) Sniff the difference between old socks and maggoty cheese.

b) Sniff men's dirty, sweaty armpits.

c) Sit by a smelly pond and sniff out foul-smelling frogs.

And, speaking of sweating, the runny wet stuff that drips from your body when it's hot is yet another amazing automatic feature.

THE AMAZING AUTOMATIC BODY-COOLING SYSTEM

Your body is programmed to keep its inside temperature at about 37°C – that's the temperature at which it runs best. When your body heats up, three million micro-engineered units in the skin produce a watery fluid known to body owners as sweat. Sweat draws heat from the blood onto the skin and, as it dries, the body loses heat into the air.

CURIOUS CASE STUDY: A NOSE FOR DANGER

The body sweats more when the brain senses danger. In the 1970s, British Intelligence body experts planned to use this fact to catch spies … with the help of *gerbils*.

The plan involved setting up fans at airports. The fans wafted whiffs from passing passengers towards a gerbil's cage. The experts hoped the gerbil's sensitive snout would sniff the salty sweat of scared spies. And then someone spoilt the secret spy-spotters' secret scientific scheme. They pointed out that innocent bodies become sweaty in airports too. The whole drippy plan proved to be a damp squib.

If the body's skin-temperature sensors detect cold air, the body has a completely different automatic programme. The body is designed to automatically twitch its muscle power units – a movement known as shivering. The muscle motors give off heat as they work and this helps to heat the body.

A MESSAGE TO BODY OWNERS...

Now you've checked your body's automatic features, you might think that it does everything for itself. BIG MISTAKE! As I said in the Introduction, human bodies need lots of looking after, and that means YOU need a care routine. But don't panic, body owners! Your *Body Owner's Handbook* is bulging with brilliant body-care hints – starting in the next chapter!

BODY CARE FOR BODY OWNERS

Most things you buy have guarantees. Toasters and tea makers, electric nostril-hair pluckers and automatic bum-scratchers come with a piece of paper promising that if there's a fault your machine will be repaired or you'll get a brand-new one. You may very well grumble – but this deal *isn't* on offer for your human body…

So you see, body owners, you've got to look after your body properly. I mean, if it breaks down, you'll find getting hold of a new body is harder than juggling custard. And that's why you really do need a body-care routine. But before we go into details, let's find out how NOT to do it…

In the bad old days before this handbook was written, some body owners dreamt up weird and wacky body-care routines. Our next curious case study is just one example amongst thousands…

51

CURIOUS CASE STUDY: HORRIBLE HEALTH HABITS!

Over one hundred years ago the Countess de Noailles inflicted her batty body-care beliefs on her adopted daughter, Maria. The Countess packed Maria off to a boarding school and made the poor girl's life a misery. Here's a letter she might have written…

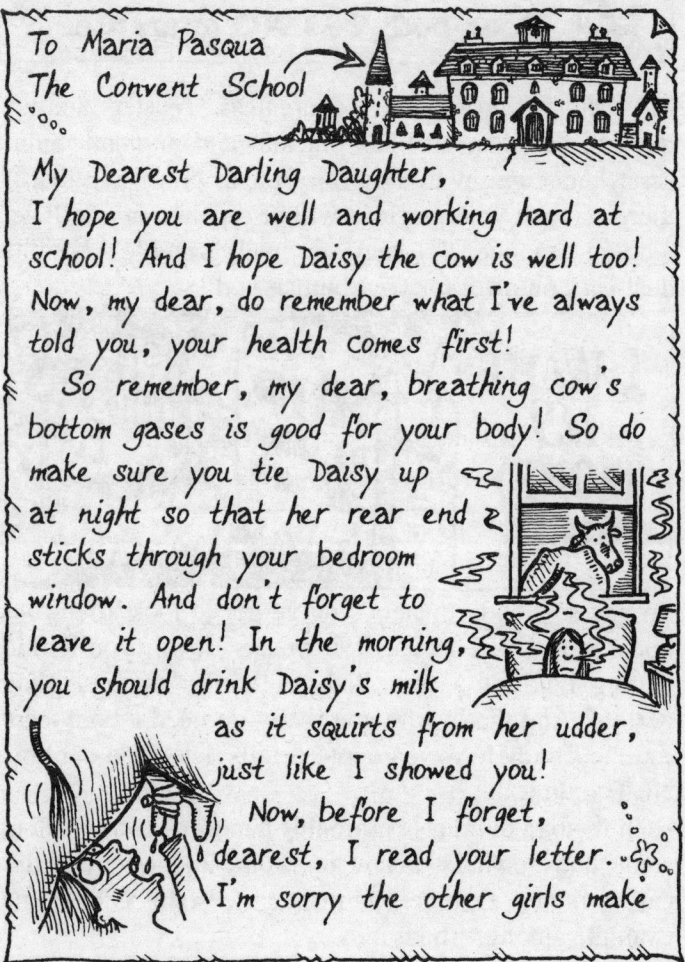

To Maria Pasqua
The Convent School

My Dearest Darling Daughter,
I hope you are well and working hard at school! And I hope Daisy the cow is well too! Now, my dear, do remember what I've always told you, your health comes first!

So remember, my dear, breathing cow's bottom gases is good for your body! So do make sure you tie Daisy up at night so that her rear end sticks through your bedroom window. And don't forget to leave it open! In the morning, you should drink Daisy's milk as it squirts from her udder, just like I showed you! Now, before I forget, dearest, I read your letter. I'm sorry the other girls make

fun of you. Yes, I did order you to go to
school dressed as an Ancient Greek!
I'm sure they'll stop teasing you
when they catch colds and you
don't because of all that healthy
freezing air blowing around your body!
Not that there's much danger, dearest,
since I've made the school drain the pond.
Ugh! Ponds! Nasty green smelly things –
just the place where germs breed!
But, my dear, if you're still
worried, the best way to keep
germs at bay is to hang onions
in your bedroom, and wrap a dead
cat's skin round your body. It worked for me!
   Well, my dearest, that's all for now, but
I'll write tomorrow with 164 more pages of
health advice...
Your Loving and Health-Conscious Mum,
   ←—The Countess de Noailles
PS And don't forget to wear your
healthy sensible open-toed sandals!

Now you might think that the Countess had a few brain
cells less than a headless chicken – and you'd be right!
But, fortunately, this handbook has all the advice you
need to take you through a whole day of sensible body-
owning....

BODY CARE TIPS FOR BODY OWNERS WAKING UP

Your body is programmed to wake up automatically at roughly the same time each day. The brain senses the light falling on its eyelids and switches to full-power mode as the light becomes brighter. You may like to try stretching your body to test its muscle motor power units and check they haven't become cramped during the night.

I always wake the Monster bright and early...

RISE AND SHINE — IT'S NEARLY MIDNIGHT!

GROAN!

Unlike humans, the Monster needs a powerful electric shock to wake him...

...followed by a body stretch!

WHIMPER!

STRETCH!

IT'S FOR YOUR OWN GOOD, MONSTER!

THE TOILET SHUFFLE

Once your body is woken up it has to be shuffled to the toilet in order to commence the liquid waste expulsion procedure known as peeing. At this point, bodies with groggy brains may forget to close the door. Human bodies are designed to squirt out unwanted pee at regular intervals and your body will have a full bladder store of pee from the night.

54

The bladder is fitted with sensors that send nerve signals to the brain as it stretches and fills up with pee. Actually, body owners should know that it's a good idea to let their body pee before the bladder gets too full. This saves the bladder from becoming too stretched and leaking at embarrassing moments.

Body data
1 Morning pee is a deeper yellow than usual because it contains several hours' worth of urea.
2 Bodies often hold their breath before they pee. This is to push the diaphragm down on to the bladder. In fact, bodies may find it hard to pee whilst taking deep breaths.

ALL-OVER BODY-CLEANING ROUTINE
Body owners don't agree on how often all-over body cleaning should take place. Some older body owners give their bodies a daily bath or shower, but certain younger body owners think that NEVER is often enough!

I give the Monster *fourteen* baths a week — he gets horribly grubby grovelling in graveyards for body bits. After the bath, a quick squirt of Monster body scent gives him that horrible "just buried" aroma ...

Eau de Coffine

In fact, the number of times your body will need all-over cleaning depends on how dirty or sweaty it gets. It's certainly useful for body owners to wash unwanted germs and sweat from their body's skin using soap and water. But soap stings the eyes and in the morning body owners should use a damp cloth to gently wipe away sleepy dust from this sensitive region.

After all-over body cleaning you should dry the area between your body's toes so that the athlete's foot fungus won't grow and damage the skin.

Body data

Body owners should not copy women in Nepal, who traditionally wash their husband's disgustingly dirty feet and DRINK the water. Well, really! Soggy cornflakes are bad enough but soggy flaked-corns sound even worse!

56

HAIR-CLEANING ROUTINE

An all-over body-cleaning session is a good time to wash your body's hair. Afterwards, the wet hair can be separated and smoothed down using a brush. Body owners shouldn't brush wet hair too hard – this splits the ends of the hairs and can turn a cool hairstyle into a frizzy fright wig…

Body data

One traditional shampoo treatment for hair includes egg yolk. This is supposed to leave hair shiny, but sulphur chemicals in the egg cause a chemical reaction and turn bleached blond hair green*!*

EAR-CLEANING ROUTINE

Body owners should take care when cleaning their body's ears. The delicate eardrum is located just a few centimetres into the earhole. The eardrum passes on sounds to the hearing system but it's easily damaged. So if water gushes into an earhole, 'ears what to do.

1 Let it dry.

2 Gently wipe the OUTSIDE of the ear with a clean cloth.

WARNING TO BODY OWNERS!

The earhole is designed to produce wax to trap dirt and invading insects. One minor body design fault is that this wax can block the ear, and it's best to ask a doctor to squirt the wax out with water.

I make the Monster's earwax into horribly tasteful yellowy-brown wax crayons, ha ha!

NOSE-CLEANING PROCEDURE

Oh dear, the Monster's lost his handkerchief. Monster, don't you DARE…!

GRRR!

PICK!

I apologize for the Monster's revolting behaviour just then! Here is the *correct* way for a well-brought-up body to clean snot from its nose.

1 Blow one nostril at a time gently into a handkerchief whilst pinching the other shut.

2 Gently wipe the nostril.

LIKE THIS… BLOW LEFT BLOW RIGHT WIPE!

58

NAIL CARE FOR BODIES

As a body owner you will need to cut your body's finger- and toenails (younger body owners may need the help of an older body owner). The correct way to cut nails is straight across so there's no danger of the nail cutting into the skin as it gets longer.

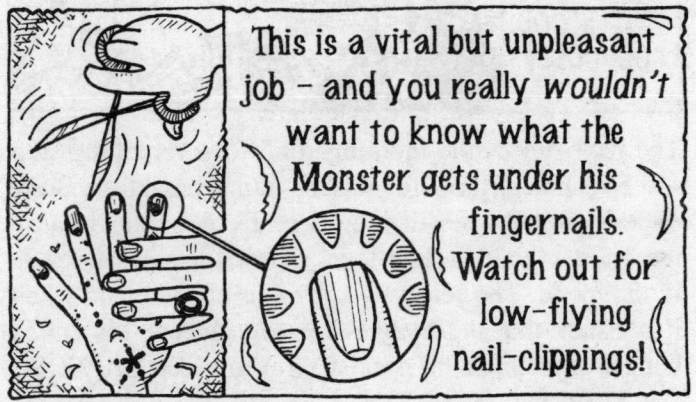

This is a vital but unpleasant job – and you really *wouldn't* want to know what the Monster gets under his fingernails. Watch out for low-flying nail-clippings!

REFUELLING YOUR BODY

Body refuelling is a vital body-care procedure and it needs to be done three times a day – in the morning, midday and evening. Without these three pit stops the body loses power, and the brain begins to run data images of juicy hamburgers and succulent pizzas – and, oh dear, the monster's dribbled all over this page.

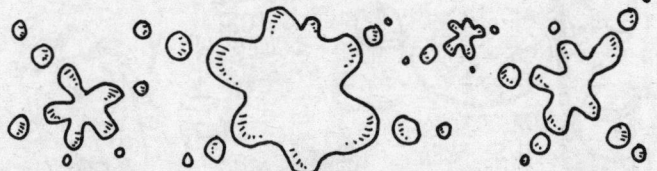

The most vital refuelling stop is the morning one: after the brain wakes up, it's groggy because it runs on a type of sugar called glucose. After a long night, the body's glucose levels are low, so you might like to try giving your body a glass of fruit juice. The juice contains glucose and a similar sugar to power up the brain.

The next step is the morning solid-food refuelling stop – the technical term for this is eating breakfast. Body owners can tell when their body needs refuelling because the brain contains a fuel-level sensor for glucose levels in the blood. The sensor is known as appetite and when it registers that the body is low on glucose it's called hunger or feeling a bit peckish or even FEED ME NOW, I'M FLIPPING STARVING!

Some bodies also consume tea or coffee in the morning. These drinks make certain body bits work faster because they contain a chemical called caffeine (caff-feen). Caffeine speeds up the heartbeat and the brain functions. But this uses up glucose and can leave the poor old bod trying to run on lower fuel levels later on.

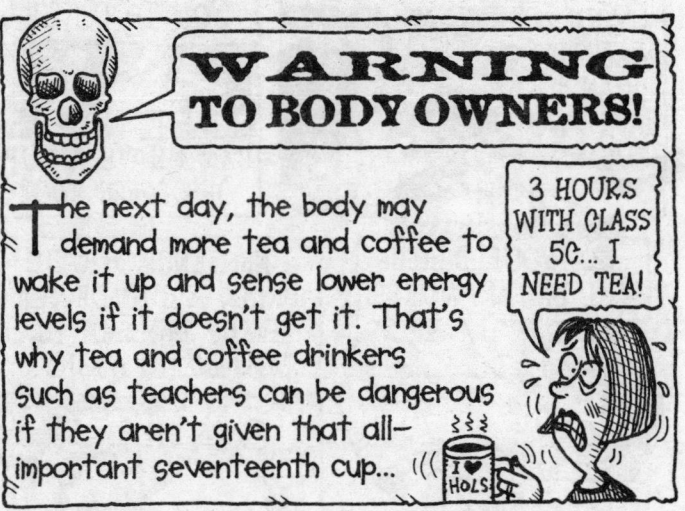

CURIOUS CASE STUDY: DEATH BY COFFEE

Body experts once thought that coffee and tea contained poisons that built up in the body. One day, Swedish King Gustav III (1746–1792) decided to test this theory on two criminals.

61

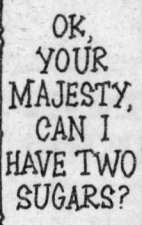

It's a fact that a few cups of tea or coffee won't damage your body, although if they're taken at night they may keep the brain awake. And caffeine does widen blood vessels. More blood goes to the kidneys and they make extra pee.

TOOTH-CLEANING TECHNIQUES

After refuelling the body it's time to clean any stray bits of food off its built-in food processors, known as teeth. This is a vital part of body care because although teeth are very good at grinding up solid food there are always bits left on the teeth. And that's not all, I'm afraid…

Even in the best-cared-for bodies, the mouth is swarming with ONE HUNDRED MILLION MICROBES. And within minutes of refuelling, the slippery microscopic monsters are greedily gobbling gobbets of food around the teeth. Worse still, the munching microbes make acid that dissolves the enamel coating protecting the teeth. They're especially fond of sweet foods and their favourite foods are those that cement themselves to the teeth to make a microbe holiday hideaway. And so, body owners, that's why you really do need to clean those teeth after fuelling your body on sweet foods.

The Monster is demonstrating the correct way to clean teeth

1 Make sure you use a small-headed soft nylon brush.

SQUEEZE!

2 Add a blob of toothpaste smaller than a pea. (I make my own "tooth" paste from ground-up teeth, ha ha!)

ACTUAL SIZE

3 Make small circular movements with the brush. Gently brush the teeth around the gums because that's where germs build up. Take care to brush the biting surfaces and the sides of the teeth. Oh, and Monster, don't press too hard!

4 Now rinse and spit.

In the basin, you bad monster!

SPIT!

WARNING TO BODY OWNERS!

Don't let your body run about with a toothbrush in its mouth. In 2001, a teacher in Cardiff, Wales, was late for college. She was in such a hurry, she was rushing and brushing at the same time. Her body fell and swallowed the toothbrush! Body mechanics in hospital cut open her stomach to remove the brush. It was nearly a brush with fate.

Bits of food can also become trapped *between* teeth. Body owners may like to try flossing away these revolting remains. Once again, the Monster has been volunteered to show us what to do…

Now listen carefully, Monster

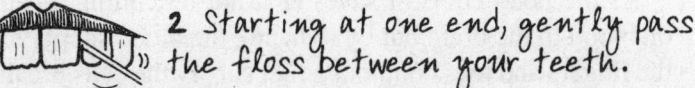

1 Take a 50 cm length of floss and wind the ends around your fingers.

2 Starting at one end, gently pass the floss between your teeth.

NEW STUFF!

3 When you've finished each tooth, wind the floss along.

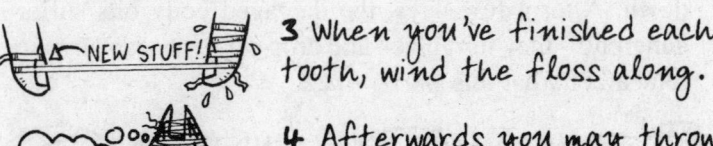

WHAT A LIFE!

4 Afterwards you may throw the floss away, or use it to tie up the cat, ha ha!

65

Hey, all you body owners out there – I bet you never knew that some mouth microbes can only live *without* oxygen? They're descended from the earliest life-forms on Planet Earth over three billion years ago! When you floss, oxygen in the air reaches them and kills them. And no, just because they've been around for a long time it doesn't mean that they should be lovingly protected and preserved in a museum. So get brushing, body owners!

Body data
A survey in 2000 showed that three-quarters of British body owners didn't know how to brush their teeth properly. And 13% of British bodies didn't have any teeth to brush, by gum!

OUT AND ABOUT WITH YOUR BODY
Body owners should always dress their bodies warmly when going outside in cold weather. And, once again, experienced body owners are correct! It really does make sense for a body to wear a hat in cold weather. You see, up to 55% of the body's warmth can be lost through the head – that's because the brain is the body's warmest part, and gets one-third of all the hot precious blood pumped up from the heart.

As the body cools, it saves heat not by cutting down on blood to the brain but by reducing the blood supply to the fingers and toes. Without a fuel supply the cells break down. After a few days, the damaged body bits suffer gangrene – they turn black and drop off. Now can anyone remember what this *smells* like?

CLUES IT ISN'T THIS... AND IT ISN'T THIS!

Such a senseless waste of Monster spare parts! Wearing a hat stops heat loss from the head and keeps the blood warm. And it saves me having to sew the Monster's toes back on, ha ha!

HAT SEWN ON TO STOP IT BLOWING OFF

It's a good idea for body owners to train their body to walk and sit with a straight spine. This is the best position to protect the curve of the back and avoid back strains. If you train your body to hold its head up – the rest of your body should take up the correct position.

HEAD UP, MONSTER!

BEFORE

That's my boy!

AFTER

As a body owner you might be more than amazed to hear that walking bodies use only 40% of their energy in walking and waste 60% in lost heat from the muscles.

(So *that's* why feet get so horribly hot and sweaty!) To use energy most effectively, your body needs to walk with its feet straight…

LIKE THIS…

RATHER THAN WADDLING LIKE A DUCK IN A DINNER-QUEUE…

CHEEK!

AVOIDING BACK DAMAGE

When your body is sitting for a long time, there's a risk of back strain. That's why you should take care to sit your body down on a chair that supports its lower back. Caring body owners could use a cushion to support this vital area…

Now the Monster will demonstrate the wrong and right way to lift a weight from the floor...

STRAIN!

THIS IS THE RIGHT WAY!

EH?

ERK!

NOW PUT ME DOWN!

BENDING THE BACK CAN CAUSE MUSCLE STRAINS THAT TAKE THE BODY A LONG TIME TO REPAIR!	**1** SQUAT YOUR BODY DOWN…	**2** USE THE HANDS TO GRASP THE OBJECT LIKE SO	**3** STRAIGHTEN YOUR BODY'S LEGS TO LIFT THE OBJECT

Body data

Female bodies can develop back problems if they walk in high heels too often. The heels cause the body to adopt an off-balance walking position that causes back strain.

BODY SHUT-DOWN MODE

Your human body needs time in shut-down mode in order to rest – body owners in the know call this "sleep", "forty winks" or "a nice snooze". Sleep normally takes place on a horizontal body recliner known as a bed. This should be firm enough to support the body's back with a firm pillow for the head (that way the head won't drop off at the same time as the body, ha ha!).

And now at last it's the Monster's bedtime...

A warm bath helps your body go to sleep by relaxing its muscles. But eating a big meal in the three hours before bedtime may keep the body awake. Once the body is asleep, only basic activities such as digestion and breathing continue. Over the next hours, the body cools by 1°C and the brain will automatically reprocess sensory information data every two hours (this is known as dreaming).

Body data

The human brain dreams in colour, but usually forgets the colours and often remembers dreams in boring black and white. Mind you, if the dream was about a penguin that turned into a zebra I expect the brain wouldn't notice the difference.

Full-sized human bodies need seven to eight hours sleep. Smaller bodies need about nine to 12 hours. Your body is programmed to spend 22 years of its life asleep (but not all at once). Sadly, this is just what happened to one young girl...

CURIOUS CASE STUDY: SLEEPING BEAUTY

This incredible case concerns a young girl named Carolina Olsson in Mönsteras, Sweden in 1876. Carolina had five brothers and they all shared a small cottage. One winter's day she came back from school complaining that she'd slipped on the ice and banged her head.

No one thought anything of it. But the girl lacked energy. Then one morning she didn't wake up! Her mother shook her shoulder and shouted, but the girl didn't move! Carolina slept all day, and she slept through the next day too. Her mother refuelled her body on milk and sugar using a long spoon. But the girl became thinner.

Carolina's family asked a doctor to look at the girl. She didn't stir. The doctor scratched his head and shouted "WAKE UP!" in her ear. Her eyelids didn't even flicker. The doctor looked grim. He took a pin and jabbed  the point hard into the girl's fingers. They bled, but Carolina didn't move a muscle! The doctor shook his head crossly and confessed that he didn't know what was wrong.

Carolina's family asked body experts at a local hospital for help but they just gave Carolina electric shocks. When these failed to wake her up, the experts sent her home again. From now on Carolina's mother kept her daughter from total body breakdown by feeding her on milk and sugar.

Weeks went by, then months and years. And all this time Carolina showed no signs of waking up. Carolina's mother and father grew older and two of her brothers were drowned in a boating accident. Carolina never knew. Then, 28 years after her daughter fell asleep, Carolina's mother became ill and passed away.

Carolina's father and three remaining sons had to work in the fields, but an old widow took pity on Carolina and came to feed her each day. Then, at last, four years later, Carolina woke up.

The old woman told her the terrible truth. *She had been asleep for 32 years and 42 days.* Her mother and two brothers were dead. Her body was now 46 years old! That night Carolina's brain was whizzing with danger signals. What if she slept and never woke up? In fact, she did sleep – but she woke up next morning as if nothing had happened!

Oddly enough, Carolina looked younger than 46 and people called her "Sleeping Beauty".

Body experts found that her body was thin but healthy. Her brain had no data from her long sleep, (that's not too surprising; when a brain is in sleep-mode the memory function is shut down). Carolina had a long and happy life, but no one knows what happened to her body to make it sleep for such a long time.

Body data
Modern body experts still can't explain Carolina's long sleep. There have been cases of human bodies sleeping for years after damaging their brains. This kind of deep sleep is called a coma, but it's rare for a body to sleep for years and then make a full recovery.

And now it's time to pull all the bits of this chapter together. The Baron has kindly supplied a checklist for all the body-care hints in these pages…

THE BARON'S DAILY BODY-CARE CHECKLIST

▶Morning: Wake up and stretch body. ▶Visit toilet. ▶Wash, bath or shower: don't forget ear care, nail care, hair care. ▶Drink to wake up brain (but not too much coffee or tea). ▶Get dressed. ▶Refuel body (breakfast). ▶Wrap up warm if going out in cold weather. ▶Out and about (don't forget how to walk and sit and lift properly). ▶Refuel body (lunch). ▶Out and about again. ▶Refuel body (supper). ▶Wash, bath or shower. ▶Go to bed. ▶Sleep.

And now it's time for your body to tiptoe into the next chapter. But, before we move on, I ought to point out that we've missed one of the most vital body-care questions. Choosing the right fuel for your body. Oh well, I'm sure you'll devour the next few pages…

NO, MONSTER! I DIDN'T MEAN EAT IT!

BOOSTING YOUR BODY

There's one thing your human body does that's truly amazing: it builds itself. Unlike every other machine on Earth, it actually gets bigger and stronger in its first 20 years! This means that clued-up body owners can create their own high-performance bodies! But first you'll need to know about the two F's, FUEL and FITNESS. Yes, read on for the full fuel and fitness facts...

FUELLING YOUR BODY

As you know, food is your body's fuel. Food energy helps your body function and grow and repair damage and move around. But what's the best type of fuel to use? There's a confusing choice of body fuels on offer...

WHERE ARE THE EYEBALLS?

No wonder body owners can get really worried about refuelling! They really do get their knickers in a twist...

AM I PUTTING IN TOO MUCH FUEL?

OR TOO LITTLE?

IS IT THE RIGHT KIND OF FUEL?

OR THE WRONG KIND?

TWIST!

KNICKERS

Hey, r-e-l-a-x! As I said, the brain's fuel-level sensor detects hunger, and sensors in the stomach tell the brain when it's full. Your body will need to consume about 50 tonnes of food in its lifetime, but not all at once!

All you do is fuel up your body when it's hungry and stop fuelling when the stomach signals that it's full. In fact, your body will feel more hungry in cold weather or when it's active because it needs extra energy to keep warm and keep moving. It's also a good idea to top up your body with water or liquid fuel. This means drinking to replace water lost as sweat from the automatic cooling system. You will probably find that your body needs more drinks in hot weather when it's soaking with sweat.

WARNING TO BODY OWNERS!

Too much water can damage the body. If a body is given more than a hundred litres in two hours, it pees non-stop and loses the vital salts it needs to send nerve signals. This can actually cause total body breakdowns, but it's very unusual.

TYPES OF BODY FUEL

You can group body fuels in the following way...

• Carbohydrate foods – contain a substance that the body can break down into glucose. This can then be used to power the muscles.

USE YOUR LOAF!

BREAD PASTA CARROTS RICE POTATOES

- Sugar-rich foods – provide an instant glucose energy fuel-boost for the body.

- Protein-rich foods – useful for building new cells as part of the body's unique self-repair and growing program.

- Fatty foods – useful for topping up the body's long-term portable reserve fuel tanks, otherwise known as fat.

- Roughage – that's fruit and vegetable skins, leaves, seeds, bran from wholemeal bread, etc. Roughage isn't a fuel but it's useful for digestion. (See page 94 to find out why, but be warned – it's a bit rude!)

Still not sure what the best body fuel is? Well, you'll need to give your body all those listed to maintain high performance. You can combine them in lots of ways – why not try making this high-quality fuel booster (also known as a snack)?

TEST YOUR BODY 4: GETTING A-HEAD

You will need:

A slice of wholemeal bread
A sliced hard-boiled egg
Some cress
A sliced tomato
Butter or margarine

IMPORTANT NOTE: Younger body owners should ask an older body owner to do the chopping and boiling and slicing. After all, the recipe doesn't need chopped, boiled, or sliced *fingers*.

What you do:

1 Lay the bread on a plate and spread a little butter or margarine on it. I say "a little" because your body doesn't need too much fat.

2 Arrange the cress as "hair" at the top of the slice.

3 Use two slices of egg as "eyes".

4 Cut a slice of tomato in half to make a sad or happy mouth.

5 Scoff the lot!

You should find:

The head contains all the food fuels your body needs. The bread contains carbohydrates, the egg has protein, the butter has fat and the bread, tomato and cress contain roughage.

Body data

In the 1980s, US scientist Bernard Heinrich decided to use science to help his body run better. He knew that bees fly miles on a drop of honey – a body fuel that's mostly sugar. So he fuelled his body on 0.6 litres of honey. Unfortunately, the honey gave his body diarrhoea and the only record Bernard's body broke was the DASHING TO THE LOO RECORD.

There! Everything a body owner needs to know about food without wasting vast amounts of money on the sort of useless reduced body refuelling schedule (known as a diet) that you find in glossy body owner's magazines…

To sum up: all you need to remember is to refuel your body three times a day on a range of body fuels. And your brilliant body does the rest! Well, that wasn't too hard too swallow, was it? And now it's time to... Oh, hold on! I'm getting loads of emails from younger body owners. It seems I've left out one terribly important fact...

Dear Body Owner's Handbook Author

Is chocolate good for my body? PLEASE TELL ME IT IS, PLEASE, PLEASE – p-leeeeeeeze!

Irma Despereet

Well, Irma, the average body guzzles 3,200 chocolate bars in its life, so this is an important question. Yes, OK, hold on, I'm giving you the answer. Please *listen*!

1 Eating chocolate makes the brain churn out powerful chemicals called endorphins (en-dorf-fins). Endorphins are usually made to block the "pain" nerve signals that the body sends to tell the brain it's damaged. The chemicals trigger the brain data programme known as happiness. So choccie cheers up the brain. Happy so far?

2 Choccie also contains caffeine, which makes the brain feel more awake, and other substances that lower blood pressure by widening the blood vessels and thinning the blood. This helps the blood flow more quickly through the blood vessels. Sounds really good, doesn't it?

3 So feeding your body PLAIN chocolate (without the fat-containing milk) about *once a week* is good for it... Oh dear!

Well, I'm sorry if you want to feed your body milk chocolate 25 times a day! Hey, don't blame me, I'm only the author! Hmm, methinks I'd better change the subject...

HOW TO REFUEL YOUR BODY

Oddly enough, after all the fuss about what kind of fuel to put in their bodies, most body owners aren't too bothered about how it actually gets *inside* their body. But body owners need to know what happens – for one thing, it can all go *horribly* wrong!

Most of the time the job is done automatically, as the Monster will demonstrate using a bowl of foul-smelling dog food that the dog didn't want...

X-RAY VIEW OF MONSTER EATING DOG FOOD

1 The Monster's teeth mash the food as spit squirts into his mouth. They work at a speed of 129 metres an hour.

2 The Monster's tongue shoves the food to the back of his mouth.

3 The epiglottis (the lid of the windpipe) snaps into place to stop the food slithering the wrong way to his lungs.

EPIGLOTTIS

4 The mushy spittle-splattered slop sloshes down to the Monster's stomach. Even if the Monster happened to be standing on his head, mighty muscle movements would force the food in the right direction.

LUNGS

STOMACH

5 The one-way trip takes nine to thirteen seconds at a speed of 61 metres an hour. In fact, the Monster could polish off another bowl of food before the first one splashes into his squelching stomach juices.

FANCY A SECOND HELPING, MONSTER?

NO THANKS!

Body data

Speed body-fuelling champion Peter Dowdeswell once downed a three-course meal – that's a pint of soup, and a huge helping of mashed potatoes, baked beans and sausages followed by 40 prunes – in FORTY-FIVE SECONDS!

COFFEE, SIR?

Body owners beware – fast fuelling can result in embarrassing gas escapes from the mouth and rear-end gas vent/solid waste ejection pipe. Rude body owners call this burping and farting. The gas is a mix of air gulped down with the hastily swallowed food, and gas made by gut microbes that feed on the food. If the food has been eaten fast, spit has less chance to digest it and there's more for the microbes to feed on and so more gas.

Fast-fuelling bodies may suffer a gush of acid from the stomach – this is known as heartburn and indigestion. Yes, body owners – indigestion is a pain in the guts!

SPEEDY HICCUPS

Fast-fuelling bodies can also suffer from a condition in which the diaphragm twitches uncontrollably – the technical term for this is hiccups. (The diaphragm pulls down to help your body breathe, remember?) Hiccups are said to happen because nerve signals are confused by fast eating. To prove this, the Baron has given the Monster a live frog to eat.

If your body suffers from hiccups it might help if it holds its breath. This allows carbon-dioxide gas to build up in the blood and slow the twitching nerves. When the Monster drinks, he holds his breath and this has the same effect…

CURIOUS CASE STUDY: HOT HICCUPS

Some methods of curing hiccups are definitely *not* recommended by this handbook! A Victorian landowner, John Mytton, tried to halt his hiccups by setting fire to his nightshirt. His body suffered a total breakdown as a result of fire damage and John's final words were:

But although body owners should beware of fuelling up their bodies too fast, the body doesn't need to chew its food for ages either. This idea was put forward in 1903 when US body expert Horace Fletcher announced (wrongly) that food-fuel needed lots and lots of chewing. To prove it he sent samples of his body's poo for experts to study. They poo-poohed Fletcher's barmy beliefs.

Body data

1 Body owners should make sure their bodies don't try to talk, sing or giggle during the swallowing procedure. This can send food down "the wrong way" resulting in embarrassing spluttering...

2 ...or choking if it blocks the air pipe. In 1994, Mexican entertainer Ramon Barrero was playing the world's smallest mouth organ when he swallowed it and choked to death. And that really was no choke, er, joke.

Now at this point you might well be wondering what happens to the food that your body has been so busily refuelling itself on. Well, if you've read this far you'll know that the guts break up chemicals in the food so they pass into the blood. (Check back to page 22 if you've just joined us.)

And from now on it all gets rather scientific. Er, so what happens next, Baron?

BODY LANGUAGE
The Baron says...

85

No, you foolish reader! ATP* is your body's energy store. The body's cells use breathed-in oxygen to turn chemicals in glucose or other foods into ATP. The body uses ATP to power its muscles and the vital chemical reactions that make the body function and grow. The process of turning food into energy is called respiration. The waste product is the carbon dioxide that wheezes from the lungs, ha ha!

* That's adenosine triphosphate (a-deen-o-sin try-fos-fate) if you really want to impress the Baron.

Thank you, Baron Frankenstein, and whilst we're talking about energy, this is a good time to introduce the topic we mentioned right at the start of this chapter. Anyone remember it? Hey, WAKE UP, body owners – boosting your body needs more than just fuel, it needs FITNESS, and you know what that means?

IT'S WAKEY-WAKEY, WORK THAT BODY TIME!

Body owners have differing attitudes to exercise. Some bodies play sports for hours and other bodies could slob-out for the Couch Potato Olympics. They seem to find it hard to tie their shoelaces without an extra-long chill-out and chocolate break.

But this handbook believes that exercise is DOUBLE-PLUS GOOD FOR YOUR BODY, and here's why. If you're using your bum-scratching machine ten times a day, sooner or later the machine will wear out. (I guess it would no longer be up to scratch.) But your body is different…

In fact, the *more* you use your body's muscles the BIGGER they get. And the bigger they get the STRONGER your body becomes! But the bad news is that taking no exercise at all makes the muscles smaller and less powerful.

BODY IN NEED OF EXERCISE

Now this handbook is NOT about how to turn your body into a super-fit athlete/footballer or whatever-you'd-like-it-to-be. As far as looking after your body is concerned, the only rule is to get as much exercise as you can and eat healthily. I'll be back in a few seconds, but first the Baron wants to say something…

I am grimly determined that the Monster wins the Annual Monster's Cross-country Race. Yes, long nights have I brooded and plotted and yet I fear the opposition! Wolfman has four legs, Big Foot's long legs match his big feet, and the Mummy is wrapped up in his training. There is nothing for it — the Monster must take more exercise to become a stronger runner. MONSTER, FETCH MY WHIP!

WOLFMAN

BIGFOOT THE MUMMY

Hold it right there, Baron!

Exercise isn't about *forcing* the body, it's about enjoyment! So why not try a new exercise on your body. How about cycling? Swimming is great since your body uses a wide range of muscles. Yes, as I said, have FUN with exercise. Unless you own a seriously sporty body, exercise is about grinning, not winning!

WARNING TO BODY OWNERS!

If your body isn't used to exercise it helps to start off slowly to avoid the dreaded cramps. This can be a sore point for some bodies.

Body data

1 Cramp is caused by a rapid build-up of a chemical called lactic acid in the muscles. The acid is made when the muscle cells try to make energy without enough oxygen. Cramps are more likely to hit tired muscles that aren't used to exercise.

2 An American scientist decided to find out how much lactic acid lizards make when they run. He let a lizard have a run and plonked it in a food blender and ... yes, you've guessed the rest. He measured the acid in the souped-up lizard. Anyone for lizard soup?

WARNING TO BODY OWNERS!

Body owners SHOULD NOT try this experiment on hamsters, stick insects, little brothers or any other small helpless creatures.

A sensible way to avoid cramps is to give your body a warm-up routine like the one the Monster is attempting…

MONSTER WARM-UP ROUTINE

To avoid straining yourself — you must begin with warm-up exercises...

Stand on your tiptoes a few times.

Now gently twist your upper body around a few times whilst keeping your legs still.

CAN I HAVE A LIE-DOWN?

NO!

Now your body's ready for some proper exercise. Let's see if it can tackle this tough test. (Er, don't worry, it's not *that* tough!)

TEST YOUR BODY 5: EXERCISE YOUR BODY … WITHOUT LEAVING YOUR ARMCHAIR

You will need:
Your body plus a friend's body.

What you do:

1 Ask your friend to read the following instructions *in any order* whilst your body tries to carry them out. How fast can your friend read and how fast can your body move?

2 Here are the instructions:

TOUCH YOUR LEFT ELBOW WITH YOUR RIGHT HAND!

TOUCH YOUR RIGHT ELBOW WITH YOUR LEFT HAND!

TOUCH YOUR LEFT KNEE WITH YOUR RIGHT HAND!

TOUCH YOUR RIGHT KNEE WITH YOUR LEFT HAND!

3 When you've had enough, swap over. You read the instructions and see how fast your friend's body manages to carry them out.

You should find:

Your body can move at quite a speed, but it's quite easy for the poor old brain to get confused by the instructions.

BEND! TOUCH! THINK! STRETCH! THINK! TOUCH!

So how did you get on? I hope your body's not too hot and sweaty and wrung out like an old dishcloth so that the stairs feel like Mount Everest. But if so, flop your body back into that cosy armchair and consider the really rich rewards of exercise...

THE REALLY RICH REWARDS OF EXERCISE

Regular exercise results in...

- Your body making more muscle cells and building bigger, stronger muscles. And your body feels stronger and more confident and walks with a better posture.

- More energy. OK, so I know your body feels tired after exercise, but after a rest your body actually has *more* get-up-and-go because its bigger muscles have more energy.

- A stronger heart – like any muscle, the heart grows stronger as it beats faster with exercise. A stronger heart means less risk of future problems. I do hope body owners take this advice to heart, ha ha!

- A brainier brain – body experts reckon that exercise makes the brain *smarter*. In some schools, children take exercise between lessons and these children score more highly in tests. A stronger heart sends a stronger bloodflow to the brain and this helps the brain to work faster and learn more.

- A good night's sleep – exercising in the evening or late afternoon relaxes your body and helps it to sleep better.

- Happiness – yes, exercise actually makes the brain feel happy! It releases those wonderful feel-good factor endorphins. So you see, exercise really is better than chocolate.

What d'ya mean you'll settle for chocolate?

Rejoice, dear readers! Thanks to exercise, the Monster is fit for the race. But is he fit to win? Time alone will tell...

A FEW NIGHTS LATER...

The bell tolled midnight. My heart beat wildly, so I put it back in its box, ha ha! The monsters took their places on the starting line...

| BIG FOOT | MONSTER | MUMMY | WOLFMAN | ZOMBIES |

The stupid zombies ran off in the wrong direction. Wolfman took the lead followed by Big Foot — Monster was last. Then Wolfman stopped to sniff a dead sheep and Big Foot stepped on a tin-tack. This left only the Mummy and sadly he began to unwind when someone trod on his bandages...

Of course, I had *nothing* to do with these accidents but I did help the Monster over the

I WANT MY MUMMY!

finishing line! Anyway ... we WON! And winning means everything to a mad scientist like me, whatever the author says!

Yeah, OK, Baron. And on that triumphant note we end this chapter ... but wait! I forgot to mention how the body gets rid of solid waste. Well, I suppose these disgusting details are important to body owners, so hold your body's nose and read on...

SOLID-WASTE EJECTION PROCEDURE

All human bodies produce solid waste. This has many names, most of which are too rude for a respectable handbook like this one.

The smelly waste is squeezed out of the rear-end gas vent/ solid-waste ejection pipe about once a day. Roughage helps the guts grip the waste and move it on faster. Bodies fuelled on foods full of roughage can produce waste up to *seven times* a day.

Body data

Actually, come to think of it, that's NOTHING! Cute cuddly pandas eat bamboo shoots full of roughage and dump it out FORTY-EIGHT times a day – yes, they really do-do!

THREE FACTS ABOUT SOLID WASTE THAT BODY OWNERS MAY PREFER NOT TO READ BEFORE MEALS...

1 An average human body spends six months of its life on the toilet. Fortunately for the average human body's family this does NOT mean six months non-stop on the toilet!

2 Most body owners are disgusted by the smell of poo – a lesson they learn when they're about two – so take a deep breath and try *not* to picture this. Some bodies have EATEN poo! In 1731, a woman *ate* a plate of poo in Paris. She washed down her disgusting dinner with some yellowish liquid that looked suspiciously like ... yes, you guessed it! She did this for religious reasons and let's *pray* that no one else does. And your family won't thank you for reading this bit aloud when the posh relations come for dinner.

3 Although poo was a subject that was left in the closet (literally), in 1994, Leeuwarden Museum in the Netherlands broke all the rules. The adverts might have looked like this...

Er, this might be a good moment to for us to make our excuses and leave this chapter. But hey, what's this?

WRIGGLE! SQUIRM! WRIGGLE!

OH NO! The maggots have escaped from page 103!

AUTOMATIC BODY-REPAIR SYSTEMS

Your body can get damaged by being knocked in some way or it can be attacked by germs. As you know, your body is designed to self-repair damage and destroy germs – but as a responsible body owner, you really do need to know what's going on.

So now's the moment to introduce this handbook's very own body-advice expert: in the village of Much Moaning, Dr Grimgrave is a much-loved local physician who can't do enough for his patients.

OK, so I got that last bit wrong! The truth is that if Dr Grimgrave was your body-advice expert you'd get the MOT – that's "Miserable Offensive Treatment"! Anyway, before we hear more from Dr G, let's take a look at a bashed-up body and find out how it repairs itself.

BODY SELF-REPAIR SYSTEMS

The Baron has kindly agreed to show us his grisly old photo album of bodywork damage suffered by the Monster. (Sensitive readers may like to read this next bit with their eyes closed!)

Ah, the sweet innocence of youth! The Monster was always getting into fights with the zombies. I've got some lovely pictures in my foul photographic albums of the injuries he suffered, ha ha!

BRUISES

When the body is knocked, blood vessels under the skin can leak blood. The chemicals in the blood break apart, first appearing dark blue before turning to lovely shades of red, purple and yellow like a glorious sunset. White blood cells gobble up the leftovers and the bruise fades.

A black eye is a bruised eyelid...

A cauliflower ear is a swelling caused by a blood clot under the skin, not a large vegetable stuck to the side of the Monster's head.

WHAT A CLOT!

When the skin is cut or scratched, the body's automatic self-healing repair service switches on. Thirteen blood chemicals form stringy fibres. These trap red blood cells and microscopic objects in the blood called platelets and create a clot.

Well, body owners, you might like to know that the clot dries to form a fresh crusty scab that keeps out germs whilst the skin underneath re-forms. The skin repairs itself from the edges of the wound, but certain younger body owners have been known to pick their body's dead crunchy scabs and chew them!

But Dr Grimgrave isn't too pleased...

Bah! This revolting habit slows the body's healing. The little clots should be served scab sandwiches for their supper!

The broken ends of bones also form clots before beginning to join together. That's why it's vital to keep broken bones straight. Once the bone has healed, special cells shape the healed area and make it as much like the old bone as possible.

Body data
In the 1990s, body mechanics in Britain were experimenting with a new glue to help fix broken bones. The substance contained blood mixed with crab poo. Claw-blimey!

SCARY SCARS
If the wound is big, the body plugs the gap with collagen. Collagen isn't skin, but as an emergency body covering it's up to the job. Mind you, it looks different and areas of collagen healing are known as scars. By the way, body owners shouldn't worry too much if their body picks up a few scars over the years. It's nice to keep your body in mint-condition but a few scars are to be expected as it's

hard for a body to avoid bumps and scrapes. Some body owners even think they give their bodies an interesting, rugged look.

Body data
Mind you, worried body owners may like to know that in 2001 scientists tested spray-on skin. The spray contained the patient's own skin cells and covered wounds to speed up healing. Let's hope they don't use spray-on furniture polish by mistake – even though it might result in a long-lasting body finish.

CURIOUS CASE STUDY: BASHED-UP BODIES
Body owners will be reassured to learn that their bodies can withstand incredible damage. For example…

1 In 1984 an American boy had nearly all his skin burnt off in a fire. Body experts regrew his skin in the lab from the few bits that were left and in the meantime the boy was wrapped in skin taken from totally broken-down bodies. He survived.

2 A Canadian lumberjack was chopping down a tree when his chainsaw slipped. He cut his WHOLE BODY IN HALF – except for nerves in his spine that take messages from his brain to his body. A helicopter rushed him to hospital and surgeons were able to sew up his broken body bits. He made it home in one piece.

One problem with serious body damage or major bodywork repair jobs like those we've been talking about is that germs can creep into the body through the wounds. This is called an infection and the body owner may notice a watery substance oozing from the area. Body experts call this pus. Pus is the result of the body's germ defence system – er, hold on, the Baron is itching to tell you the disgusting details…

> Ah, the sweet smell of fresh pus! Pus is an interesting mixture of liquid from blood, dead white blood cells and dead germs. Smelly brown pus means a serious infection, when limbs may need to be chopped off, ha ha! But a little pus seems to get the body's defences to work harder and the wound heals faster.

PUS ON PUSS

A NOTE FROM THE AUTHOR

The Baron has just offered to show us his book of home remedies. He says that he's tried most of them on the Monster, but I'm not sure if Dr Grimgrave approves of this sort of thing…

GRRR! THIS BOOK IS UTTER HOGWASH!

FATHER

BARON FRANKENSTEIN'S SECRET BOOK OF CURES

LICKING WOUNDS

When bloodied in a fight, all animals lick their wounds. The water helps to wash out dirt and the spit contains germ-killing substances. Sadly these do not kill all germs which is why the mouth oozes with microbes and I am told that doctors don't advise spitting on wounds.

LICK!

HARMFUL MICROBES

TO CLEAR UP AN INFECTED WOUND

Pour a small bucket of squirming maggots over the wound. Ah, my little wriggling friends! Maggots devour rotten flesh and help with the healing. Modern doctors use maggots and the Australian Ngemba tribe traditionally used bandages dripping with blood and maggots for the same reason. How intriguing!

WRIGGLE!
MUNCH!
SQUIRM!
DON'T LEAVE THEM ON TOO LONG!

> Note to myself: I must remember to use blowfly maggots on the Monster. African tumbu maggots burrow into flesh. They may be removed by leaving bacon on the skin and yanking the maggots out when they come out to feed. Oh well, it might save the Monster's bacon, ha ha!
>
> TIME TO COME OUT!

Fortunately, if your body is unlucky enough to be attacked by germs you don't need to rely on the Baron's rotten remedies. The automatic germ-destroying system is ready and waiting...

THE AUTOMATIC GERM-DESTROYING SYSTEM

Wide-awake readers of this handbook will know that skin and snot and tears form part of the body's defence systems. But if germs get inside the body they're zapped by the body's super-complex white blood cell defence system. Here's how it works...

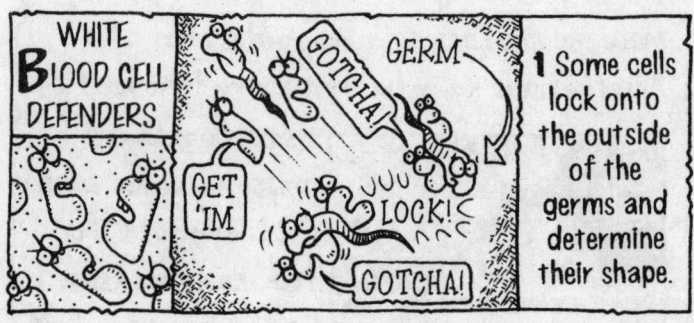

WHITE **B**LOOD CELL DEFENDERS — GERM — GOTCHA! — GET 'IM — LOCK! — GOTCHA!

1 Some cells lock onto the outside of the germs and determine their shape.

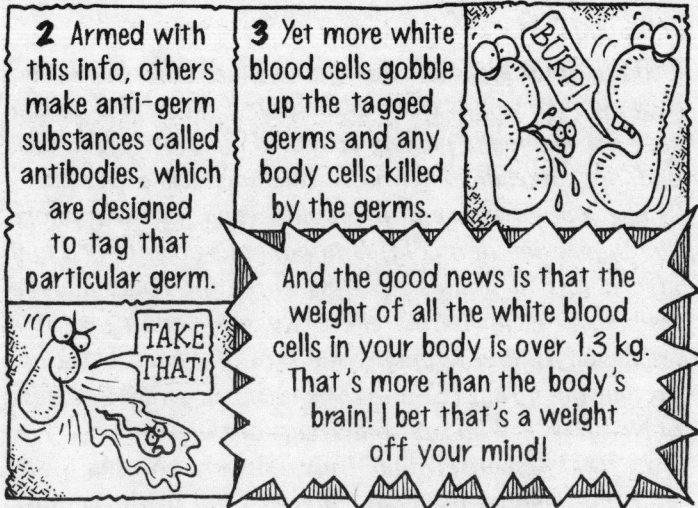

2 Armed with this info, others make anti-germ substances called antibodies, which are designed to tag that particular germ.

3 Yet more white blood cells gobble up the tagged germs and any body cells killed by the germs.

BURP!

TAKE THAT!

And the good news is that the weight of all the white blood cells in your body is over 1.3 kg. That's more than the body's brain! I bet that's a weight off your mind!

DISEASE ATTACKS ON SMALLER BODIES

Some smaller bodies get clobbered by any disease that's around. This is because their body defences aren't too good at fighting off germs. In fact, small bodies often pick up diseases from their local germ factory (sorry, I mean *school*).

Fortunately, small bodies are tough and recover quickly. Their anti-germ defences even grow stronger because some white blood cells can "remember" the germs and attack them next time. And so the poor protesting pupils are packed off to school all too soon…

In 2000, Italian body experts claimed that dirt is good for smaller bodies. So getting to grips with germs by mud-pie making, being slobbered by the dog, kissing the cat, and licking fluffy lollies off the floor, trains white blood cells to remember germs so the body can fight off disease. Younger body owners could try this excuse next time their bodies get dirty…

Who says "grime doesn't pay"?

Body data

1 *Bodies pick up colds when germs get on their hands and they put their hands close to their nose. Nose-picking is a sure-fire method of picking up a cold. Your body feels sick and, of course, anyone who is watching feels even sicker.*

2 *The only treatment for colds (and flu – a more violent version of a cold) is to put your body to bed and give it lots of liquids. Useless cures for colds include rubbing pork fat on the chest (Russia – don't take this for grunted), and wrapping the skin of a dead black cat around the throat (USA – remember the crazy Countess of Noailles?). Who says black cats are lucky?*

3 *In 2000, scientists at the University of Nebraska, USA, said that feeding the body chicken soup helps the nose make extra snot. Since snot is part of your body defences, chicken soup is good for colds. Mind you, I still think it tastes fowl.*

OK, body owners, I hope you're getting the message: your body is designed to heal itself. But that hasn't stopped body owners from inventing DIY healing methods. These methods were as sensible as putting your pet poodle in a python's cage and saying, "Hope you guys don't mind sharing!" But the Baron's an old-fashioned mad scientist and he's a great believer in dodgy old folk remedies. Oh dear – time to check out the old cure book again…

BARON FRANKENSTEIN'S SECRET BOOK OF CURES:

HOW TO TREAT A SORE THROAT USING PEE

There are two schools of thought about this. I think it works, and everyone else thinks it doesn't. Gargling with hot fresh pee is an ancient Chinese remedy. I tried it on the Monster once and he's never complained of a sore throat since!

PEE

NOT AS POTTY AS YOU MIGHT THINK

NAPPY RASH

WAAAH!

DON'T BE TEMPTED TO STUFF NAPPY INTO BABY'S MOUTH

In southern USA, one traditional treatment was to wipe a rash with a baby's pee-soaked nappy; they even wiped their faces! How very refreshing!

HOW TO SOFTEN EARWAX

Dribbling drops of hot pee into the earhole was a traditional treatment for hard earwax in ancient China. The hardest part was holding the Monster's head still long enough...

DON'T BE A DRIP!

PARDON?

I am afraid Dr Grimgrave isn't too impressed by these treatments:

CURIOUS CASE STUDY: A WEE DROP

The urea in pee is poisonous in large doses and it tastes terrible but that didn't stop pee drinkers. In the 1970s, Indian Prime Minister Moraji Desai drank a glass of his pee a day – so was he a potty Pee-M? Some people thought so! Phil Heath of Britain was another pee drinker. In the 1990s, he gulped down a glass a day. He said it tasted terrible but he still drank his Phil and used the rest for washing his body.

ORDERING SPARE BODY PARTS

When body bits break down or get damaged beyond repair, surgeons can remove the worn-out body bits and stick in spare parts from broken-down bodies. In fact, hospitals can get hold of replacement hearts, livers, kidneys, and even hands. I expect they come from a "second-hand" shop.

No, seriously, these spare parts are often given away freely once a body is beyond repair. But in the USA in 2001, body bits were sold for money. Here are some actual body bit prices from that year. You may be amazed at how much a broken-down body is worth!

HONEST JOE'S USED BODS

YOU NEVER KNOW WHEN YOU MIGHT NEED THEM!

One cornea (the see-through bit of the eyeball)	£2,500
One set of bones	£19,500
0.37 square metres of skin	£26,000
Pick 'n' mix box of leftover body bits	£98,500
TOTAL COST OF BITS	£146,500

(Genuine body bits — one careful owner!)

WARNING TO BODY OWNERS!

Body owners, you are STRONGLY WARNED against selling your body bits, especially when your body is still in working order! Taking out your body's vital bits and swapping them with bits from other bodies can cause serious body breakdowns!

If you don't like the idea of bits from another body being put into your body, there is an alternative – use a machine designed for the job. Body experts are also developing ever-improved mechanical replacement body parts including joints, voice boxes and hearts.

BODY OWNER'S REPAIR QUIZ

So you've read this chapter and you think you know everything there is to know about body repair. But which of these so-called body repair facts (supplied by the Baron) are just too incredible to be true?

TRUE or FALSE?

1 It's possible for your body to make blue snot.
2 Hitting your body's head causes it to see stars.
3 Reading wears out your body's eyes.
4 Injecting your body with pee helps it to fight germs.

Answers:

1 TRUE (in theory). Some bacteria are blue and snot oozing with the bacteria would be blue too. But you might see it once in a blue moon (or do I mean once in a blue hankie?). By the way, green snot gets its lovely colour from a germ-killing substance containing iron made by white blood cells.

2 TRUE. The fantastic flashes are the body's retina light sensors switched on by the force of the blow and firing nerve signals to the brain. Body owners shouldn't try thumping their bodies to see stars – try using a telescope instead!

3 FALSE. Reading for hours in dim light strains the muscles that keep open the pupil – that's the hole that lets light into the eyeball. But no amount of reading can wear out the eyes. So your body can eyeball the rest of this handbook without any worries!

4 FALSE. But in 1990, a doctor in California, USA, got into trouble for injecting his patients with pee and making this claim.

So how did you do? Are you fit to be a body expert or is your state of knowledge rather sickly? Either way, you'll find plenty of riveting reading in the next chapter. It's about fixing bust-up, broken-down bodies – and it's *you* doing the fixing!

BODY BREAKDOWNS AND RECOVERY

The human body is designed to last a lifetime, but as Dr Grimgrave is sure to remind us, what can go wrong will go wrong. And sometimes the body's own self-repair systems need a helping hand. To find out what body owners can do and what needs expert help, here's a series of terrific trouble-shooting charts with Dr Grimgrave's advice on how body owners can deal with common body problems. Thanks, Doc!

GRR – DON'T CALL ME "DOC"!

TROUBLE-SHOOTING CHART 1: THE HEAD

PROBLEM: NOSEBLEEDS	POSSIBLE CAUSE	DR GRIMGRAVE'S TREATMENT
	A broken blood vessel caused by: **1** High blood pressure – this may happen if the brain gets over-excited. OVER-EXCITED!	My bleeding patients are forever causing problems - especially the children, they're little bleeders!

CONTINUED →

112

2 Dry air damaging the wall of the nose's blood vessels.

3 Explosive nose blowing or nasty nose-picking by body owners.

BLAST!

PICK!

Pinch their nostrils and lean them forward for a few minutes.

They shouldn't blow the nose for a couple of days or they'll blow their chances of healing.

Flaking of head skin cells due to an infection by microbes.

Use an anti-dandruff shampoo.

DRUFF STUFF

An idiot once asked me how you catch dandruff. "In a paper bag!" I replied.

Body data

In 1994, a shampoo called "Dander-Ban" was dander-banned in Uruguay, South America. The anti-dandruff shampoo was just too powerful – it left hundreds of customers completely bald! That must have been a hair-erasing experience...

TROUBLE-SHOOTING CHART 2: THE DIGESTIVE SYSTEM

PROBLEM	POSSIBLE CAUSE	Dr Grimgrave's treatment
DIARRHOEA	Diarrhoea is usually caused by an infection of the guts. The body tries to rid itself of the germs by emptying the food tube (guts) using the rear-end gas vent/ waste ejection pipe. MESSAGE FROM BOTTOM... STANDBY TO EJECT!	This condition sorts itself out. Patients should rest and drink liquids so they don't dry out. LIQUID IDIOT After all, drying out can lead to dying out, ha ha!
CONSTIPATION	**1** When the brain is upset, the poo is held up in the guts and dries hard as the gut sucks out water. SUCK! SUCK! SUCK!	Eating more fibre causes more waste to be made quicker - so it's pot lucky, ha ha! PLOP!

CONTINUED →

PROBLEM

CONSTIPATION

2 Another cause is lack of roughage, which slows food and poo down as it moves through the guts.

(HE'S SITTING ON THE LOO)

BRAN FLAKES (ROUGHAGE)

URGH!

Laxatives make the patient produce waste, but I keep my surgery toilet locked. When the laxatives work it's amusing to watch the patients make a fast exit!

LOO

VOMITING

Vomiting happens when the stomach ejects its contents. This may have many causes. Fear, gut infections and foul food can all produce this revolting result.

VOMIT!

Every vomiting body should drink a sweet drink in small sips to avoid drying out.

SIP!

Of course, vomit can be fascinating to study - see my case notes. I always keep a jar or two of vomit to study over dinner!

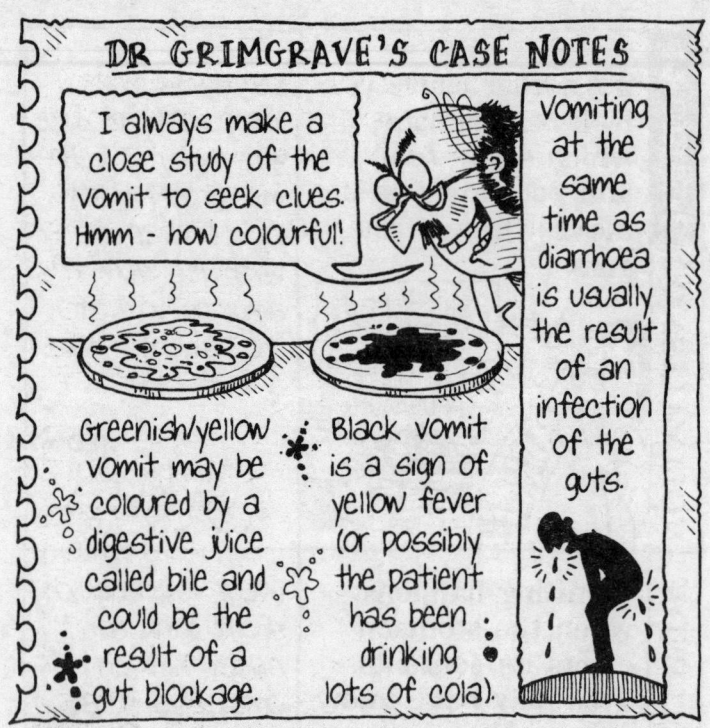

CURIOUS CASE STUDY: IT'S TOUGH ON THE THRONE

King Ferdinand I of Naples (1751–1825) had chronic constipation. When the straining sovereign found the going tough, he invited a crowd of friends into the Royal toilet to keep him company. The Austrian Emperor Joseph (1741–1790) was one of them:

WE MADE CONVERSATION FOR MORE THAN HALF AN HOUR AND I BELIEVE HE WOULD STILL BE THERE IF A TERRIBLE STINK HAD NOT CONVINCED US THAT ALL WAS OVER.

BAFFLING BODY CHANGES

Eventually, young human bodies start to change in a strange fashion. Now, as you're about to find out, this isn't really a body breakdown, but it sometimes feels like one to the bewildered body owner. The body may sprout hair in unusual places. (This isn't new hair because human bodies have more hair than chimps, remember? But each hair is longer and thicker than before.)

Anyway, do you know what that means? No, silly, they're not turning into werewolves! It's worse than that – they're turning into *teenagers*!

Dear reader, I have a puzzling problem. The Monster is acting in a freakish fashion. He is becoming horribly hairy. He even has three wispy hairs on his chin that he proudly shaves each day. His muscles are getting bigger. He's friendly with those brainless young zombies, and he's taking an unusually close personal interest in the Vampire. What in the name of horror is happening?

THE VAMPIRE'S HORRIBLY PRETTY...

DON'T WIND ME UP!

HIS VOICE SOUNDS DEEPER.

WAS IT LOVE AT FIRST FRIGHT?

BLUSH!

Body data

1 Blushing is a basic body reaction. It happens when the brain runs a feeling-embarrassed program. The brain squirts a chemical into the blood that makes the blood vessels widen under the skin and turns fair skin red. It's always "glowing" to happen at the wrong moments for teenage bodies.

2 A teenage body's voice sounds deeper because the vocal cords that make the sounds of the voice are getting bigger. Large male bodies have bigger vocal cords, so they make deep, gruff, growling sounds.

Becoming a teenager is a pre-programmed body-changing process that often takes several years. Girl bodies turn into women and boy bodies turn into men. Girls often start to change about two years before boys. At this point girls may become taller than boys – but the boys catch up.

Meanwhile, a girl's ovaries and a boy's testes squirt chemicals called hormones into their blood. (*Hey, who says teenagers are lazy?*) A boy's hormones make bigger muscles and his body appears more hairy. Hormones make a girl's body have periods, grow hair in private regions and become more curvy.

Body data

A little hormone goes a long way. Imagine that the water in your local swimming pool was the blood in a teenage body (yes, I know a real pool full of blood would look horribly messy and you wouldn't want a swimming lesson in it). But if the swimming pool was the body's blood the hormones would be no more than a pinch of salt.

Now, let's look at some teenage body problems…

TROUBLE-SHOOTING CHART 3: COMMON PROBLEMS IN TEENAGE BODY MODELS

PROBLEM	POSSIBLE CAUSE	DR GRIMGRAVE'S TREATMENT
BODY STINKS	Teenage and adult bodies ooze oily sweat around the armpits and rude bits. Munching microbes feed on the gungy grease and make sickening smells.	Regular clean clothes and a good wash with germ-killing soap.

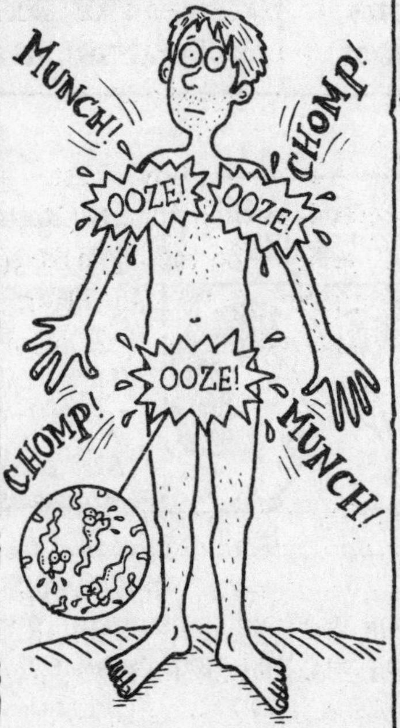

MUNCH! CHOMP!

OOZE! OOZE!

OOZE!

CHOMP! MUNCH!

EEK! WE DON'T WANT TO LEAVE THIS LOVELY SMELLY ARMPIT!

ERK! ARGH!

I won't be making any amusing remarks about body odour because this type of humour stinks!

CONTINUED

119

BAD BREATH

"EEK!"

Caused by germs. It's made worse by a dry mouth (not drinking enough water), failure of the body owner to clean their teeth, smoking or drinking alcohol or eating onions or garlic. Pfwoar!

Rinse out the mouth with mouthwash and clean the teeth - or suffer a nasty "brush" with your dentist.

If a patient has bad breath and smelly feet, it's probably foot and mouth disease, ha ha!

BODY LANGUAGE

I STUDY HALITOSIS (HALLY-TOE-SIS).

YOU LOOK AT HAYLEY'S TOES — YUCK! WHO IS HAYLEY ANYWAY?

Answer:
No, it's worse than that! The body expert studies bad breath – halitosis is the posh body expert's jargon for a manky mouth.

Body data

1 Teenagers aren't the only body types that suffer from bad breath. All bodies get it – but teenagers are the most scared of it. Especially when they're meeting their boy- or girlfriends. Body owners should be warned that their body is designed to spend two weeks of its life in lip-puckering, sloppy snogging!

2 One traditional cure for smelly feet involved stuffing bran into socks to soak up the sweat. It didn't work, but at least you could make your own crunchy cheesy-bran breakfast cereal.

START YOUR DAY ON THE RIGHT FOOTING!

CHEESY BRAN

CURIOUS CASE STUDY: A LOW-DOWN DIRTY CROOK

In 2000, a robber held up a bank in San Diego, USA. It seems everyone held their noses rather than sticking their hands up because the man was so *smelly*! Hmm, he sounds more like a "rank" robber! Police helicopters blared loudspeaker warnings about the smelly man. Soon afterwards, a nosy motel receptionist noticed a nasty niff from a new guest. She called the cops. A good detective follows his nose and that's just what the cops did – the man was soon arrested and "scent" to jail. He should have taken a bath – he'd have made a clean getaway!

The Monster is excited because the Vampire has invited him to her tomb. But this morning a terrible scream rang from the bathroom. The Monster has pimples, or zits as young persons call them! His face looks like a dot-to-dot puzzle!

I told the Monster that 80% of teenage bodies suffer spots. They are caused by the body over-producing oily fluids to protect the skin. This is caused by those lovely hormones. The spots form as the skin's oil tubes are blocked and infected by gruesome germs. I fear the Monster was not paying attention. He was moaning in panic and trying to squeeze his pimples. AARGH! That spurt of pus hit my eyeball!

That young idiot is making his spots worse! If germs from his fingers get into the spot it will become even more infected. He should wash the oil off his hair and skin each day and use an anti-spot fluid and cleansing pads. Meanwhile, if the young fool wants to go on a "date", as young persons call it, he should wear a paper bag over his head. Pleasure's too good for the young, you know.

GRIMGRAVE
1942

WORRISOME WARTS...

And talking about skin problems, warts have attracted more than their fair share of freaky folk remedies. Who better to reveal all to us than a certain mad scientist with his secret book of cures?

BARON FRANKENSTEIN'S SECRET BOOK OF CURES

REMEDIES FOR WARTS

I am of the opinion that a few warts improve a face but as usual everyone else disagrees! That's why I am plotting to try these traditional treatments on the Monster if he ever gets warts...

> IS THAT THE BEST YE CAN DO?

THE DOG'S PEE TREATMENT ~ The pee was smeared on the warts. This was a popular Tudor treatment - well, I don't think it was popular with anyone with warts, ha ha! If this didn't work, the sufferer could always try rubbing the warts with pig's blood oinkment, er, ointment.

THE DEAD SLUG ~ Get a fat slimy slug from the garden and crush it and smear the mashed-up slug-juice all over the warts. If this doesn't work you could catch a grasshopper and make it gnaw the warts with its strong jaws.

> THIS SHOULD DO THE TRICK!

123

THE CAT'S TAIL TREATMENT

You need to stroke the warts with a tortoiseshell cat's tail during the month of May. Hmm, I wonder where I can find such a cat? Do I have to cut its tail off?

NO! YOU DON'T!

THE DRIBBLE TREATMENT ~ You dribble over

the warts first thing in the morning. I am told that in Kansas, USA in the 1990s,

WARTS WRONG WITH YOU LOT?

children who suffered from warts were taken to church. After prayers, a woman known as "the wart lady" licked the children's warts with the tip of her tongue. Hmm, even I think that sounds cruel!

I wonder if any of these treatments work? Obviously not, judging by Dr Grimgrave's reaction…

BAH HUMBUG! BALDERDASH! CODSWALLOP!

ACHING ADULT BODY MODELS

The owners of full-sized adult body models often try to tell smaller body owners how to look after their bodies. Much of this advice is sound and sensible but it should be pointed out that some adult body owners don't look after their own bodies too well. Fuelling the body on too much alcohol, tobacco and drugs causes MAJOR body problems. Who says that adult body owners are *always* right?

Read this next bit or regret it later…

DANGEROUS DRINKING, SMOKING AND DRUGS

1 Alarming alcohol

The human body doesn't need alcohol and doesn't want alcohol – even if the body owner is gagging for it! Alcohol soaks into the blood via the stomach and then the liver has to remove 28 grams of alcohol every hour. This means the body can drink a small glass of beer in one hour and not get drunk. Any more alcohol escapes into the blood and affects the brain for a few hours.

Now, my dear readers, I would like to tell you the story of how alcohol affected the Monster at the Zombie's Halloween Party…

Midnight: Monster's first drink. At this stage the Monster looks fairly normal…well, normal by his standards, ha ha!

12.30: Monster's third drink.

Alcohol dries the germ-killing spit and causes smelly breath.

Red face as alcohol widens blood vessels under the skin.

1 a.m.: Monster's fourth drink.

I ROAM GRAVEYARDS, I DIG UP BODIES, I SCARE VICARS... IT'S A REAL SCREAM...

YAWN!

Alcohol weakens hearing — making the Monster talk louder. The befuddled Monster thinks he's being funny when he's actually being boring.

2 a.m.: Monster's sixth drink.

I GESH THESH NO RESHT FOR THE WICK –HIC –KED...

Alcohol confuses the brain's speech systems.

Clumsy actions due to alcohol affecting the brain's movement controls.

Wider blood vessels mean more blood goes to the kidneys. The kidneys make more pee.

ER – S'CUSE ME!

Alcohol upsets the stomach causing vomiting.

The morning after the night before...

I WANT TO DIE!

YOU'LL HAVE TO COME ALIVE FIRST!

Alcohol dries out the body causing headache, tiredness and sickness. This stage is known as the hangover.

An idiot thought my surgery was a pub and said he felt like a bottle of wine, so I told him to put a cork in it, ha ha! In fact, one or two alcoholic drinks aren't harmful - I've been known to indulge in the odd glass of wine after a hard day dealing with idiots. Small amounts of alcohol may reduce the danger of blood clots in blood vessels.

TERRIBLE TOBACCO

Some body owners reckon that smoking is cool and grown-up and daring. OK, so why don't they jump off a cliff? It's definitely daring and it could be less risky to their body's health. Take a close look at what's in these cigarettes...

NEW HAPPY PUFFS

WITH ADDED...

...NICOTINE (POISON)

...TAR (POISON)

...CARBON MONOXIDE (POISON)

YOU'LL BE GASPING FOR THEM!

Yes, you spotted it. ALL THESE SUBSTANCES ARE POISONOUS. That's right, they all harm the body! Like most doctors, Dr Grimgrave holds firm anti-smoking views…

> Anyone who smokes should be allowed to smoke as much as they like - just so long as they're on top of a bonfire, ha ha! One of my idiot patients, Mrs Ashtray, smokes and is overweight. Yes, she's a heavy smoker. This woman is a school dinner lady. She smokes in the kitchen and flicks her disgusting ash into the boiled cabbage and custard. This causes the children to vomit over their teachers, and the head-teacher isn't brave enough to tell her off.

Smoking causes bad breath. If you want to know how bad try kissing an ashtray…

I SAID AN ASHTRAY NOT *MRS* ASHTRAY!

HELLO, DUCKS!

PATIENT RECORD: STRICTLY CONFIDENTIAL

NAME: Mrs Ashtray

DIAGNOSIS: Mrs Ashtray suffers from smoking. The effects are obvious:

Wrinkled skin caused by tobacco poisons killing cells. <u>Brown teeth</u> (tobacco stains). <u>Loss of teeth</u> caused by <u>gum disease</u>.

PROGNOSIS: she is in danger of... <u>Strokes</u> due to <u>blood clots</u> forming in the brain and damaging the control systems for muscle movements. <u>High blood pressure</u> which can cause <u>blindness</u>. <u>Breathlessness</u> caused by <u>lung damage</u>. <u>Diseases</u> of her lungs and breathing passages. (Some smokers lose their <u>diseased tongues</u>.) Fat building up around the heart causing <u>heart attacks</u> (this is caused by nicotine). <u>Diseases of her guts and bladder</u>. <u>Painful legs</u> due to <u>narrowing blood vessels</u> and shortage of oxygen to muscles. <u>Blood clots</u> that may cause her arms and legs to <u>rot</u>. Some smokers end up having their arms and legs <u>cut off</u> in extreme cases.

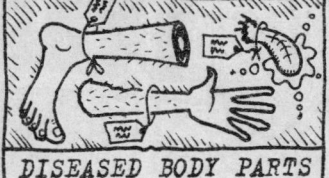

DISEASED BODY PARTS

ADVICE: Give up smoking AT ONCE!

I ought to point out that these are just the NICER effects of smoking. Doctors believe that each cigarette takes five minutes off the length of a body's life.

The trouble is that Mrs A is gasping for nicotine. Within ten seconds nicotine makes the brain feel calmer and more alert, so going without nicotine can be very hard. That's why smokers want to smoke even if cigarettes get so expensive it's cheaper to smoke banknotes. What a pity! The earlier smokers give up smoking, the more chance they have of avoiding all those nasty diseases!

So Dr Grimgrave has decided to be cruel to be kind. He's had a word with the Baron. And the Baron (who is kind of cruel too) has agreed to take away Mrs Ashtray's cigarettes and lock her in his dungeon until she agrees to give up smoking *for ever...*

DANGEROUS DRUGS

An important message to body owners...

There are a lot of dangerous drugs around, but body owners only need to know *three* things about them...

- All banned drugs are poisonous in large amounts.
- The trade in banned drugs is controlled by cold-hearted criminals who aren't nice people to give money to. Why not pay to help fluffy little kittens and playful puppies? They're far more deserving!
- No one has ever found lasting happiness by taking drugs. Many have found lasting unhappiness and some have found even more long-lasting death.

WHINGEING WRINKLIES

As time goes by, owners of older bodies grumble more and more about their body's faults and problems. It's a sure sign that their bodies are beginning to wear out. Body experts call this process ageing and it's horribly complicated – but Dr Grimgrave's latest book explains everything...

IF YOU'RE AN IDIOT –
YOU'LL LOVE IT!
(HEALTHY TIMES)

ONLY AN IDIOT WOULD BUY THIS!
(DAILY STRETCH)

The Idiot Patient's Guide to Health

By Dr H. Grimgrave
(author of Diseases I have known)

CHAPTER 14
AGEING

IT'S ONLY A MATTER OF TIME, YOU KNOW

Ageing is something that affects every body in time and there's no cure for this condition. I have drawn a diagram to make this clear in a way that even my most idiotic patient can understand...

Body cells contain DNA (that's deoxyribonucleic (dee-ox-ee-rye-bo-new-klay-ick) acid for all the non-idiots amongst you). DNA is a kind of chemical blueprint for building the body and it's found in all body cells.

CELL

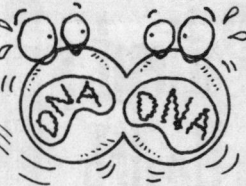

As cells divide in order to make new cells their DNA starts to get damaged and wears out.

Chemicals called free radicals are made when the cell makes food into energy. These chemicals also damage DNA.

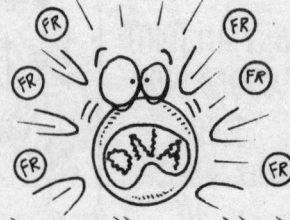

When the DNA is too damaged to work, the cells die. As the cells die off, the body appears to age. Old age creeps up on us all, you know. Why, even my colleague Dr Sneak has taken to wearing slippers and a cardigan and drinking cocoa when he's off-duty.

DEAD CELL

DNA

TOTTER!

WOBBLE!

Body data

Yes, I know that DNA damage from making energy is a major design fault, but this shouldn't stop you feeding your body in order to keep it working. Hey – wait a moment! Trust Dr G to leave out the good news! Body owners can't stop their bodies ageing, but they can slow ageing down*!*

1 Taking lots of exercise slows the loss of muscle cells. This helps to keep the body in good condition in its later years.

2 Choosing the right food also helps. Chemicals called antioxidants soak up nasty free radicals and defend your body's DNA. These crucial chemicals include vitamin C in fresh fruit and vegetables and vitamin E in wholemeal bread and brown rice.

So, body owners, it helps to be keen on greens and nice about rice.

A message to adult body owners...

Adult body owners will be thrilled to hear that red wine contains antioxidants! I bet some body owners will be so keen to get the health benefits that they'll open a few extra bottles to make sure they're getting enough! Don't forget the problems of drinking too much alcohol (see page 125).

And now let's look at some of the problems that bodies encounter as a result of ageing. Can Dr Grimgrave offer any hope of putting them right? Thought not...

TROUBLE-SHOOTING CHART 4: OLDER BODY MODELS

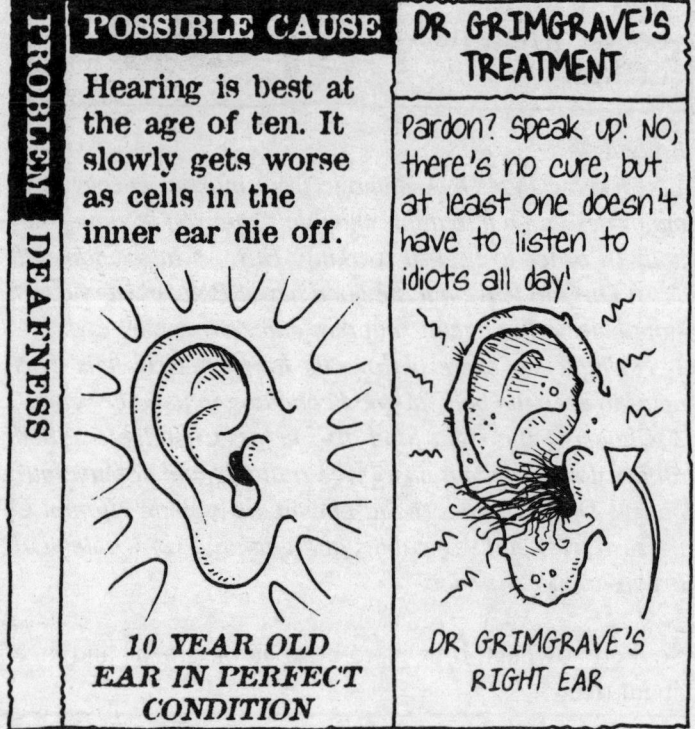

PROBLEM	POSSIBLE CAUSE	DR GRIMGRAVE'S TREATMENT
DEAFNESS	Hearing is best at the age of ten. It slowly gets worse as cells in the inner ear die off.	Pardon? Speak up! No, there's no cure, but at least one doesn't have to listen to idiots all day!
	10 YEAR OLD EAR IN PERFECT CONDITION	DR GRIMGRAVE'S RIGHT EAR

BALDNESS

All bodies lose hair as they age as a result of cells dying off. But balding in males (like noses) can run in families.

1962 1982 2002

There is no cure for this condition so don't waste my time. GRRR!*

DRY MOUTH

Older people make less spit due to a loss of cells in the spit production units in the mouth.

THOSE WERE THE DAYS!

Lack of germ-killing spit results in more mouth microbes and bad breath and wind.

The wind has the same cause as wind due to fast eating on page 83. Patients with this problem are ordered to wait outside!

CONTINUED →

135

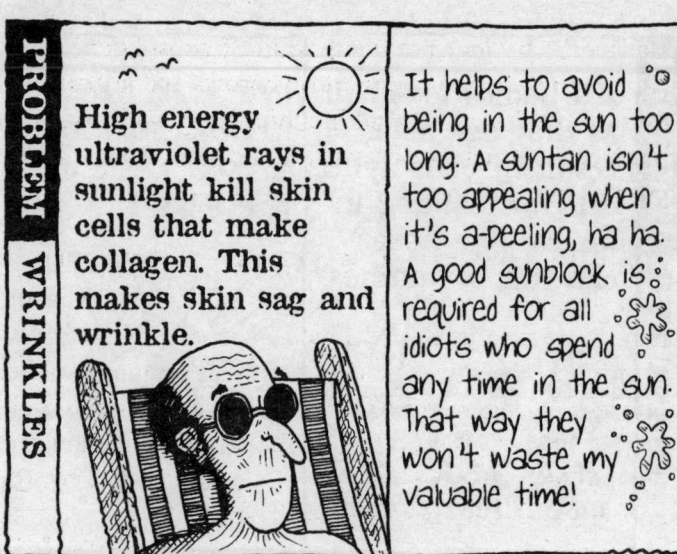

High energy ultraviolet rays in sunlight kill skin cells that make collagen. This makes skin sag and wrinkle.

It helps to avoid being in the sun too long. A suntan isn't too appealing when it's a-peeling, ha ha. A good sunblock is required for all idiots who spend any time in the sun. That way they won't waste my valuable time!

*By the way I should have warned you that Dr Grimgrave is a bit touchy about his own baldness.

BODY LANGUAGE

A body expert says...

I SUFFER FROM ALOPECIA (AL-OH-PEE-SEE-AH)

IS THAT WHY YOU'RE WEARING A STUPID HAT?

Answer:
Correct! It's what body experts call balding. Oh well, it's hair today, gone tomorrow. Oh dear, I don't think Dr G appreciates my little joke.

But the body *does* provide a kind of consolation prize. Hair begins to sprout from the eyebrows and nostrils and ears – isn't that nice? And in a lifetime a male body can produce two metres of nostril hair. Now where did we put that electric nostril-hair plucker?

CURIOUS CASE STUDY: BALD, BAD AND BRUTAL

Tsar Paul (1754–1801), Emperor of Russia, was the none-too-proud owner of a bald-bonced body. This was a seriously sensitive subject. One day a stupid soldier pointed at the sovereign's slap-head saying, "Look, there's baldy." The cruel Tsar heard the comment and ordered his guards to flog the soldier to death (I bet the poor man bald, I mean bawled, really loudly).

Next, power-crazed Paul banned the word "bald" from dictionaries and announced that anyone who dared to say the word would be executed.

You'll be pleased to hear that the ruthless ruler was killed by his soldiers and today Russians can use the B-word without fear of death.

BODY OWNER'S BALDNESS-CURE QUIZ

For many years the owners of balding bodies have seen the loss of head hair as a major design fault and have tried to put it right. Our fearless Horrible Science artist volunteered to try the Baron's traditional treatments.

Sorry, Tony! Anyway, all you have to do is match each substance to the treatments below...

Substance used:
1 Horse pee.
2 Cowpat.
3 A dead rat.
4 Green tea, honey and monkey bladders.

Treatment:
a Drink it.
b Eat it.
c Put it on the scalp.

138

A note to younger body owners...

It's hard to discover a teacher's age without asking the body owner – and risking some terrible teacher torture. To make matters worse, female body owners may pretend their bodies are newer than they are. But here's a way to prove that your teacher's body isn't 25 years old (like she's been claiming for the past 30 years).

TEST YOUR BODY 6: HOW ANCIENT IS YOUR TEACHER?

You will need:

An ancient teacher body (if you can't find one, an ancient non-teaching body will do).

A small body (ideally from the same family but you can use any body).

What you do:

1 Compare the length of their ear lobes.

2 Compare the length of their teeth.

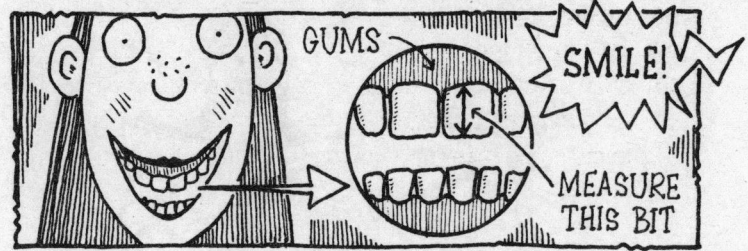

You should find:

1 Older bodies often have saggy ear lobes. They get longer during the body's life and the force of gravity pulls them downward.

2 The old saying is right – older bodies really are "long in the tooth"! Ageing makes the gums shrink and the teeth appear longer.

A message from the author

Vintage bodies should never be written off. Many of the problems described above are quite minor faults and a well-cared-for body of advanced years is still capable of many years of useful service.

And there's one thing that older bodies are very good at – looking after newer bodies. Well actually, the next chapter is about the care and workings of these little bodies. But I must warn you that they're wild and savage and not properly potty-trained! So you should read on at your own risk!

BRAND-NEW BODIES

Human bodies do more than walk and talk and pee and poo and sleep and dream. They're also designed to produce *more* human bodies. Just think about it! You may own a TV, but I bet it can't turn into *two* TVs! And that automatic bum-scratcher isn't going to make you a new one in a million billion years. But human bodies are actually *designed* to make brand-new human bodies, or babies as they're commonly known!

Of course, this is very technical and advanced stuff for body owners, but fortunately we have our experts to guide us. The Baron has just built a baby out of body bits. He's calling her "Little Monster". Here she is now with her proud creator…

LITTLE MONSTER, STOP SUCKING THAT THUMB AND PUT IT BACK IN THE JAR WITH THE OTHER BODY BITS…

Of course, body owners shouldn't try to make babies from body bits – you see the body is programmed and designed to do the job without cutting any bodies up.

HOW THE BODY MAKES A BABY

The first thing that happens is that a human body pairs up with another human body. Two adult human bodies are needed (one male and one female – they're often described as parents). It helps if the bodies in question are:

a) Alive.

b) In love with one another.

At this point the body owners ask themselves if they're willing to feed the new body and love it and look after it in the years before the brand-new human body (baby) is able to look after itself.

The two adult bodies are fully equipped to make the baby. The female (known as the mother) produces a tiny DNA-containing micro-production unit – an egg. The egg comes from one of two high-tech assembly and storage units called ovaries. The male (often referred to as the father) makes millions of smaller micro-engineered DNA delivery units known as sperm in his testes. Each sperm is designed to carry a copy of the male's DNA to the egg.

X-RAY VIEW OF EGG FACTORY (FEMALE)

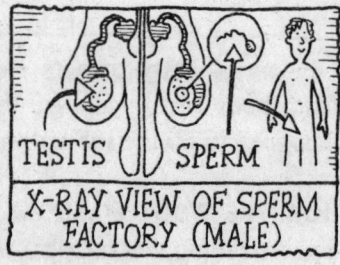

X-RAY VIEW OF SPERM FACTORY (MALE)

Body owners can let their bodies get down to the mingling of sperm and egg with (hopefully) lots of fun and romance and love sensations running in their sensory

142

equipment. But, since 1978, it's also been possible for scientists to do the necessary mixing in a less romantic test tube.

THE INCREDIBLE EGG AND SPERM RACE

Body owners are sure to be interested in what happens inside the female's body once the sperm gets there. Basically, the sperm do what they're designed to do: swim to the egg. For the sperm, it's a tough long-distance marathon. It's like a full-sized body swimming 11 km – that's 1,375 lengths of a large swimming pool. Let's see how this one's getting on…

Our sperm beats its little tail and races about 70 million other sperm. It's hard work – it takes 1,000 tail beats to get 1 cm and there are dangerous white blood cells to dodge on the way. Hey, keep going little guy!

Body data

Allowing for the size difference, the human body can't swim as fast as a microscopic sperm. A strong swimmer can manage 11 km per hour but some sperm race the equivalent distance in a few minutes. Only about 100 sperm make it to the egg. But 69,999,900 don't – they die. The surviving sperm squirt chemicals that dissolve the egg's protective wall. The egg is about 1,000 times

143

bigger than them – so it's a bit like alien tadpoles burrowing into a big squidgy asteroid. But, at last, our sperm triumphantly dives inside.

It's so excited, bless it, that its little tail falls off.

Now it's time for the vital body-planning session. Over the next few hours the entire appearance of a new human body is hammered out. What's happening is that the sperm and egg combine their DNA to make a blueprint for the new human being. Let's hope they agree on the details!

Body data

German body expert Paracelsus (1493–1541) claimed you could make a body without a soul by mixing sperm and horse dung for 40 days. Hmm, this would explain sinister scientists, dangerous dinner ladies and terrible teachers. Well, it would if it had worked.

All you body owners reading this might well think that making a new body sounds horribly complicated – and you'd be right! But in fact we've only reached the *start* of a nine-month process. This ends only when the new body is released from its development capsule in the female – this is known as being born. To tell us what happens Dr Grimgrave has found the relevant chapter of his book…

The Idiot Patient's Guide to Health

CHAPTER 12

MAKING BABIES

A SIMPLE GUIDE FOR SIMPLE PATIENTS

I'm writing this chapter to stop my patients bothering me with idiotic baby questions. Anyone would think I'm here to help them! In fact, I do *not* approve of

 babies. They are messy and noisy and they often suffer from vomiting and diarrhoea and this results in even more noise and mess.

Why anyone should want to make a baby is beyond me! There are more interesting things for an intelligent person to do like studying rare diseases and collecting human body parts! However, babies are being made in shockingly large numbers. In the past few **MINUTES** about 1,600 have

been delivered and by the end of today
there will be around 250,000 – and about
90 MILLION in a year's time! That's an
awful lot of extra work for long-suffering
doctors like me!

FROM EGG TO BABY

WEEK 1

I will not go into the business of how eggs
and sperm join forces – I believe any idiot
knows about that. Sometimes two eggs
meet with two sperm to make two twin
bodies. More rarely, a developing egg splits
into two eggs to make two bodies with the
same DNA blueprint – they're called
identical twins. Dreadful thought! Double
the trouble and double the expense!

Afterwards the egg (or eggs) puts down
roots in the part of the female's body
known as the womb (we doctors call it the
uterus). The egg feeds off
the female's body – making
chemicals to dissolve some
of the womb cells and using
them as food to grow. Of
course, the little brats expect
free food for ever after that.

UTERUS

The egg is now dividing
into new cells and these cells
are dividing every two days.
This may not sound very
dramatic but in 20
divisions an egg will turn into ONE
MILLION cells. A nine-year-old human

DIVIDE!

child growing at this rate would be over 10,000 metres tall – that's higher than Mount Everest – in just *thirteen days*. What a nightmare! One idiot patient claimed her boy had grown an extra FOOT this year, so I told her to knit him an extra sock, ha ha!

WEEK 5

HEART

EAR ARM

EYE

LEG

By this stage the baby's heart is pumping. Of course, it's rather small, no larger than a grain of rice. So it's not too heavy for the mother to curry, er, carry.

WEEK 7

The baby's eyes are now operational. It can detect a red glow from the light shining through its mother's body. The baby also forms fingers and toes. Oh well, that's a handy feat, ha ha!

WEEK 8

The baby is now the size of a hen's egg. I will not attempt an amusing remark since I do not approve of "cheep" laughs.

GROW! GROW! GROW! GROW!

WEEK 9

As the baby continues to develop, its guts, as vulgar persons call them, begin to make digestive juices. The baby is now being fuelled though a tube from its mother and floats in a watery bubble. If older children were kept in bubbles and fed through tubes they would be far less naughty. Not a bad idea in my opinion!

We doctors call the baby's all-purpose feeding and life-support system the placenta (pla-sent-ta). The mother's blood can't get to the baby but the placenta supplies all the vital chemicals and food the baby needs, and removes waste from the baby's blood. It does all this in just 30 seconds! If only I could get rid of my patients this quickly – sigh!

WEEK 11

If there are twins developing in the womb, after 11 weeks they kick and punch one another. Time for discipline in my opinion!

Body data

Actually Dr G hasn't mentioned that the following week they make friends and kiss and hold one another. It's TRUE. In other words if your body happens to have a twin – the two bodies had a fight and made it up before they were even born!

Now back to *The Idiot Patient's Guide to Health…*

WEEK 12

Babies have no sense of hygiene. They perform bodily functions whenever they feel like it and expect their parents to clean up after them. In fact, this disgraceful behaviour begins *before* they are born. By week 12 the baby is making

148

urine, or pee as vulgar persons say, in its water bubble. Harumph, the baby should tidy its own womb! Unfortunately the baby is also *drinking* its water, including its own urine. *Disgusting!*

WEE! SLURP!

WEEK 13

The baby's developing brain is now able to hear sounds through its developing hearing system. Of course, it's even less intelligent than an idiot patient, but it's developing 250,000 brain cells a minute. My patients seem to be *losing* them at the same rate.

WHADDYA MEAN, LESS INTELLIGENT THAN AN IDIOT PATIENT?

WEEK 14

The baby sleeps most of the time, which is surprising given the noise its mother makes – her thumping heart, puffing lungs and gurgling guts. Of course, some people are annoyingly noisy. On occasion I have had to be quite rude to patients who insist on screaming in agony during minor surgical operations.

ARGH!

DR.GRIMGRAVE

WEEK 16

By this week the baby is able to hiccup. An idiot patient had the hiccups after swallowing a camera film. I told her to ring me if anything developed, ha ha!

WEEK 19

Idiot patients might be confused to learn that by this week the baby's body is covered in hair! It's the only time the little brat might suffer all-over dandruff, ha ha!

WEEK 20

Like most children who visit my surgery, unborn babies find it impossible to stay still. Instead of waiting quietly to be born these idiotic babies play silly games. They perform somersaults and kick and frown and touch their faces and wave their arms and open and shut their mouths. It's all attention-seeking in my opinion.

OPEN! FROWN! SHUT! WAVE! KICK!

WEEK 21

By now the mother's body is getting uncomfortable. The selfish baby is insisting on growing even if it squashes the mother's insides. Even her heart and lungs are squashed and she gets a little breathless and suffers from back strain. But I suppose we shouldn't blame the baby – it's a normal result of making babies, I'm afraid.

PUFF, PANT!

Meanwhile, the mother's body is having to work harder to supply the baby's body. Her lungs need to handle 20% more air and her heart and kidneys are coping with 50%

more blood. As her bladder gets squashed she keeps needing to go to the toilet. Well, no one said that having a baby was easy. "No gain without pain", that's what I always say!

WEEK 26

The baby's body hair has dropped out now. Sadly, a similar thing seems to have happened to my head hair! And so I don't want to hear any amusing remarks from readers on *that* subject!

WEEK 28

Even though it hasn't been born, the baby is able to recognize the sound of its mother's voice. Pah! Any idiot can do that in my opinion.

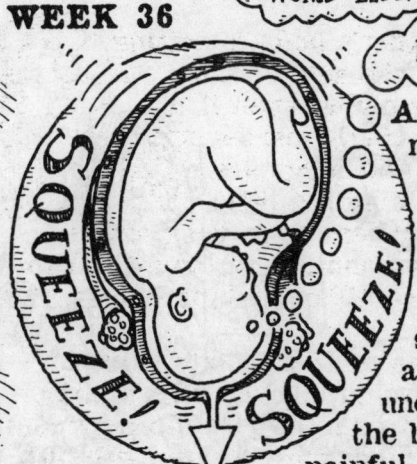

NOT MUCH "WOMB" LEFT!

WEEK 36

I'M OUTTA HERE!

SQUEEZE! SQUEEZE!

At last the womb muscles begin to squeeze and the baby is forced out. This process may take several hours and can be uncomfortable for the baby and painful for the mother.

Pah! Anyway, as a doctor, I have helped to deliver many new babies. The main thing is to keep the baby warm — the tiny little brat can't shiver yet. It is also necessary to cut the feeding tube. The cut end will drop out. I am currently looking for preserved tubes for my medical collection if any reader happens to have one lying around...

BODY LANGUAGE

Dr Grimgrave says:

Do you say...

Answer:
NO! The umbilicus is yet another bit of posh body expert's jargon. This word means the hole where the feeding tube joined your body – you might call it a belly button.

Being born is tough for the baby. As soon as it emerges from its mother it's got seconds to rearrange the blood flow around its heart and fill its lungs' air inlet/exhaust system with air and not water. If it doesn't manage this it suffers a total body breakdown. Thankfully, nearly every baby makes it. And there it is – a brand-new human body in full working order!

The baby's first view of the world is deeply scary. Apart from the shock of seeing its parents for the first time (that must be *really* scary!) it can't see properly. A baby's brain can't handle vision yet and it sees double – that's *two* sets of parents – both upside-down! No wonder newborn babies cry!

153

Body data

New babies produce green poo. They haven't pooed for nine months and the green colour comes from a build-up of bile digestive juice made by the liver. Older body owners should make sure their bodies eject waste more often than this. And now let's see what Dr Grimgrave has to say about babies...

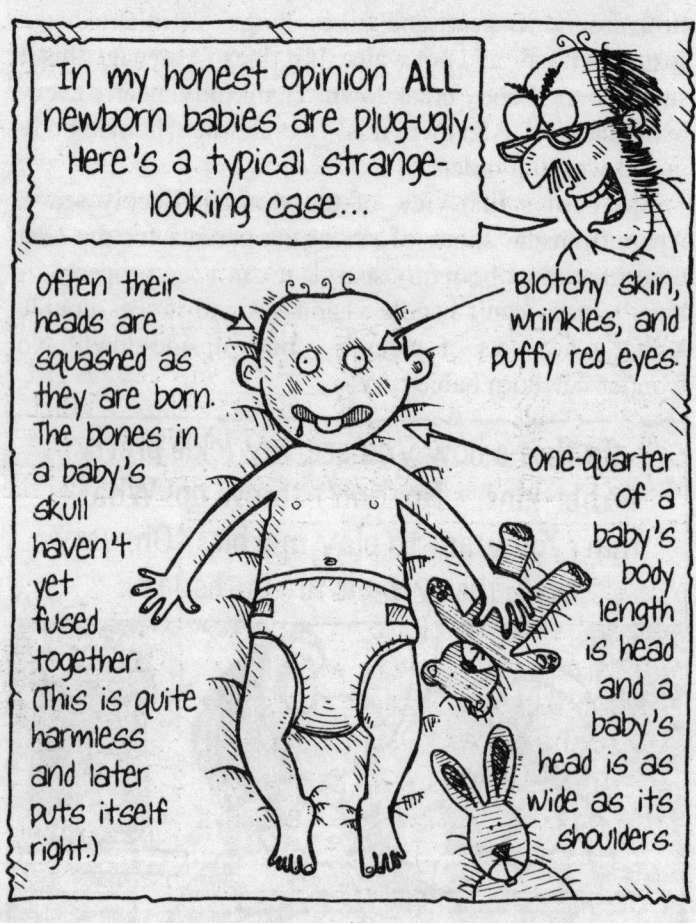

If one of my idiot patients looked like that the other patients would scream and run a mile, leaving me with a nice empty waiting room. That'll be the day - sigh! But doting (dotty) parents have a totally different reaction...

DOTING, DOTTY PARENTS

Body data

In fact, brains (apart from Dr Grimgrave's) always find baby faces cute and appealing – it seems the brain is programmed this way. They also get wound up by the sound of a baby crying as Little Monster is about to show us…

OK, SO YOU DON'T WANT TO PLAY WITH THE EYEBALLS - WELL WHAT IS WRONG, MY LITTLE MONSTER-KINS?

I find all this silliness and nonsense deeply depressing. It will all end in tears of course - usually baby tears. Babies cry when they want things - usually a cuddle or to belch or break wind (or fart as some rude persons say). Most often it's because they want a feed, the ill-mannered little brats...

155

In fact, adult female bodies are equipped with a built-in portable refuelling system for hungry babies. It's so good it sells itself…

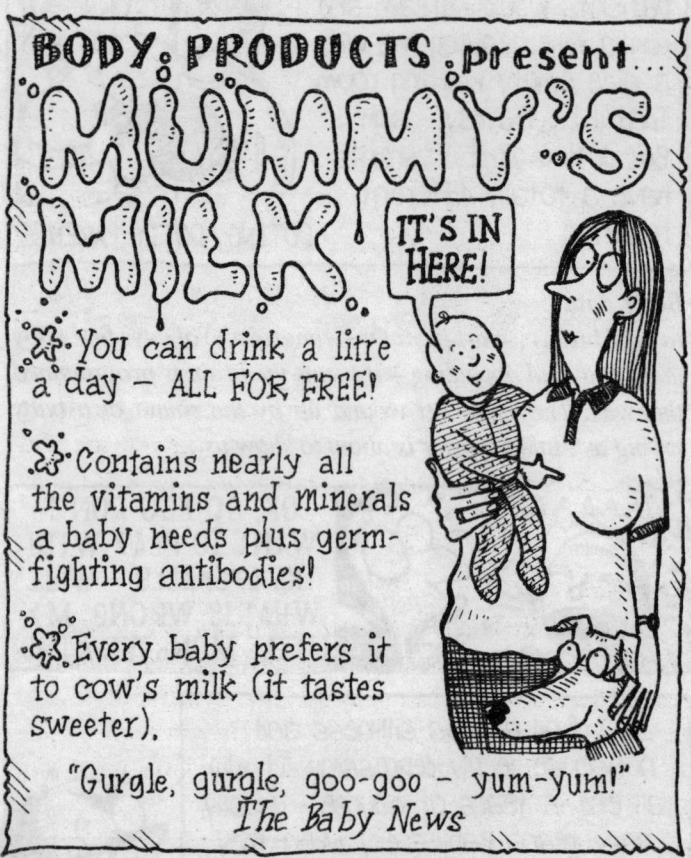

At this stage in the chapter, body owners might be wondering what use babies really are. After all, what do they actually do? Eat, sleep, burp, poo, pee? Wrong! Baby bodies are programmed by their DNA to develop and change 24 hours a day – and NOTHING is going to get in their way…

For example, at birth the new human body is just one-twentieth of the weight of a full-sized human body, but its weight is designed to increase *four* times in two years. In two years, the baby body will have crawled 150 km and self-programmed its brain with the correct data and balance control to allow itself to walk.

Actually, walking is harder than it looks because it involves learning how to use 200 muscles in the right order, but brilliant babies take it all in their stride and they go on to do something no animal body in history has ever managed ... they talk!

Body data

1 In the 1970s scientist Herbert Terrace tried to teach a baby chimp named Nim to use sign language. Like a human baby, Nim learnt to be naughty and use a potty, but he only learnt 125 word signs in four years. Human baby brains store over 1,500 words in the same period. So poor Nim proved to be more of a chimp than a champ.

157

2 And the human brain goes on to store thousands more words. Well, that's handy because your body chatters on for a lifetime total of ten years, remember? Now that really is something to talk about! And of course knowing lots of words and what they look like on a page has helped your body to read this book for you.

Well, body owners, your *Body Owner's Handbook* is almost over. We just have time for the final chapter – now where did I leave it?

What's that, Little Monster? You did WHAT on it? Oh well, I suppose I can dry it off...

A FINAL NOTE TO BODY OWNERS

As you've just found out, being a body owner is a full-time job. Despite its incredible automatic features, your body really does depend on you to work properly. In fact, that's what this whole handbook has been about, making friends with your body!

Improving your body should start when it's still fairly new and growing because this is when giving the body the best fuel and exercise has the most effect. But even a battered old banger of a body can be improved by a bit of tender loving care and the right bodywork treatment, so here's your ultimate…

BODY OWNER'S HANDBOOK ADVICE
- Give your body plenty of exercise to build the powerful muscles and lungs and heart that will keep your body going strong for a long lifetime. And regular exercise helps to postpone ageing in full-sized bodies.
- The more your body's brain practises a skill the better it gets. The more work the brain does, the faster and smarter it gets.
- Giving your body the right food builds a strong body that lasts even longer. This means fuelling it on a range of fresh food and lots of fruit and vegetables with those amazing antioxidant goodies.

159

No body comes with a guarantee, but a cared-for body lasts longer. There's no way in a million years your body can run like a cheetah, climb like a gecko, swim like a seal, fly like an eagle or hear like a bat. But your body is fit for millions of other jobs and its power is limited only by the size of the imagination program in its amazing human brain! And best of all, the body is all yours – FOR LIFE!

BODY OWNER'S HANDBOOK

QUIZ

Now find out if you're a
Body Owner's Handbook expert!

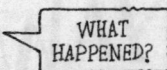
WHAT HAPPENED?

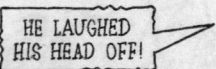
HE LAUGHED HIS HEAD OFF!

Basic Body Maintenance

Attention body owners! If your body's central information processing unit (otherwise known as the brain-box) has been switched on during this book you ought to know how to get the best from your human body. Have a go at the quiz below and see if you can spot the correct body care tips.

1 Why is it important to drink plenty of water?
a) Your bizarre body is mostly water and needs topping up regularly
b) Because the oxygen in water is absorbed into the blood stream
c) To wash the poo through your guts as quickly as possible

2 How many hours sleep should young bodies get a night?
a) Two or three is fine – young bods have more energy than old ones
b) 9 to 12 hours are enough to make sure you don't nod off in your Science lesson
c) At least 12 – young bods use up a lot of energy during the day and need plenty of sleep

3 What is the most effective way of keeping your teeth clean and avoiding horrible halitosis (that's bad breath to you)?
a) Small circular motions and just a tad of toothpaste
b) Up and down with a good squeeze of toothpaste
c) One big bag of peppermint creams a day will keep you minty fresh

4 Why should you sit up straight in your Science lesson?
a) To stop you falling asleep
b) To keep your bonce properly balanced and aid thinking
c) To avoid straining your back

5 What is the best way to trim your tough toenails?
a) Straight across – keep it simple
b) Curved to the shape of your toe – keep your little piggies pretty
c) Just tear them off with your teeth

6 And while we're flirting with feet … why is it important to dry thoroughly in between your toes?
a) To stop skanky skin flakes building up
b) To stop you slipping around in your socks
c) To stop foul fungus sprouting up

7 Which part of the body gives off most heat?
a) Your bottom – that's why they invented thermal underwear
b) Your head – make sure you keep your noddle warm with a hat
c) Your feet – wear two pairs of socks to keep your toes toasty

8 Which of the following can result from stuffing down food too fast?
a) Embarrassing bottom burps
b) Disgusting diarrhoea
c) Sickeningly sweaty armpits

Answers:
1a; 2b; 3a; 4c; 5a; 6c; 7b; 8a

Astonishing Organs

Your body's organs keep your body machine going – without them even the simplest functions like peeing or important ones like ... well ... breathing would be out of the question. Find out if you've really got to grips with your inner workings by matching the awesome organ with its job in your bod.

1. Controls everything – from blinking to beating up your baby brother

2. Squirts out disgusting digestive juices to break down food into the crazy chemicals that keep your body ticking over
3. This odd organ kills off unnecessary red blood cells, but you can live without it

4. Keeps your gloopy blood whooshing around your body

5. Collects and stores pee to avoid embarrassing leaks at the wrong moment

6. Sucks in air to get important oxygen into your body

7. Stores all the fantastic food substances that your body needs to function

8. Fundamental filtering system to keep your system clear of unwanted chemicals and water

a) Lungs

b) Heart

c) Kidneys

d) Spleen

e) Liver

f) Brain

g) Bladder

h) Stomach

Answers:
1f; 2h; 3d; 4b; 5g; 6a; 7e; 8c

Making Sense of Your Senses

From your all-seeing eyeballs to your tingling taste buds, your senses help your body machine make sense of the world. But not everything you hear or see (or taste or touch) is quite what is seems. Have a look at these strange statements and use your common sense to work out which are sensible and which are senseless.

1 Your amazing body comes equipped with five super senses: sight, smell, taste, touch and hearing.
2 If you sneeze with your eyes open, your eyeballs will plop out and roll across the room.
3 Your sensitive skin is the heaviest human organ.
4 Girls smell better than boys.
5 Your brilliant brain makes you blink to stop too much light entering your eyes.

6 Your tingling tongue can detect five flavours.
7 You can't taste things when you have a cold because if you have no sense of smell you have no sense of taste.

Answers
1 SENSELESS. Actually strange scientists can't agree about how many senses there are. Some people think that things like pain and balance are also senses.
2 SENSELESS. You should know by now that your body's better put together than that. Strong muscles hold

your eyeballs firmly in place.

3 SENSIBLE. You might not think of skin as an organ, but it is. And it makes up around 16 per cent of your total body's weight!

4 SENSIBLE. This is true in all senses (ha ha!), but scientists have proved that girls' nifty noses are more sensitive than boys'.

5 SENSELESS. Blinking helps keep your eyeballs clean with tears – your eyelids are like weeny windscreen wipers.

6 SENSIBLE. The five basic types of taste are sweet, salty, sour, bitter and umami.

7 SENSELESS. Taste and smell are two independent senses, so scientifically one doesn't affect the other. But the smell of food does affect your experience of it, so when you have a stuffy nose the fabulous flavour of food might seem different.

The Digestion Ride

As a responsible body-owner, you'll know how vital it is to regularly fuel your body with food. But what happens to your bite of soggy sandwich? Fill in the missing words as you follow the food on its rollercoaster ride through your body.

The disgusting digestion ride begins in your **1**_____, where your slimy sandwich is chomped up by your teeth and dissolved by **2**_____. When it's all soft and sticky, grisly globs of your sandwich pass down a long tube into your **3**_____. Here your muscles churn it all around like a giant washing machine, shooting out **4**_____ to turn it into a semi-liquid. The runny gloop that was once your sandwich is then squirted into your **5**_____, where some of it is absorbed into your **6**_____ and other bits that haven't been squished and squashed and digested enough are turned into **7**_____. Any liquid leftovers from your sandwich are passed out as **8**_____. Just think – this is all happening inside you as you complete this quiz...

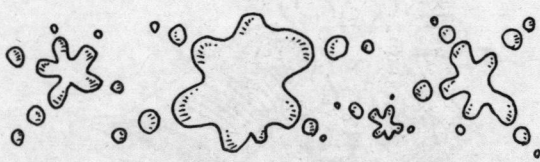

a) Intestines
b) Poo
c) Stomach
d) Mouth

e) Pee
f) Blood
g) Saliva
h) Juices

Answers:
1d; 2g; 3c; 4h; 5a; 6f; 7b; 8e

Beastly Blood

Where would your body be without its blood supply? This fantastic fluid is permanently pumping round your body, carrying chemicals and destroying deadly diseases. Take this quick clue quiz to find out all about the liquid of life. But be warned – it's not for the squeamish.

1 Which incredible organ keeps your brilliant blood moving around your body? (CLUE: This awesome organ takes some beating)

2 What type of blood cell attacks grisly germs that get into your body? (CLUE: They're fine fighters, all white)

3 Which gas is lugged around by your red blood cells? (CLUE: You'd be breathless without it)

4 What colour are red blood cells without this gloomy gas? (CLUE: They may be a bit depressed without it)

5 What are the tubes called that blood travels through in your body? (CLUE: This is a crafty question)

6 What brilliant body bits in your blood help it to clot? (CLUE: Perhaps they look like little pieces of crockery…)

7 What crazy chemical element is common in your beastly blood? (CLUE: Heavy metal)

8 Which blood type can be given to anyone – whatever their own type – in an emergency? (CLUE: Oh – you know the answer to this)

Answers:
1 Your heart
2 White blood cells
3 Oxygen
4 Blue
5 Blood vessels
6 Platelets
7 Iron
8 Blood type O

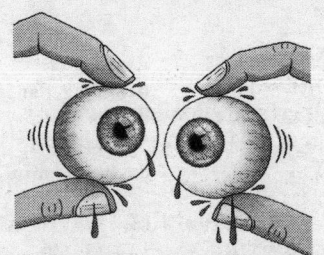

HORRIBLE INDEX

171

172

173